Earth Tales

from Around the World

Michael J. Caduto

Illustrated by
Adelaide Murphy Tyrol

fulcrum resources

Fulcrum Publishing
Golden, Colorado

Library of Congress Cataloging-in-Publication Data

Caduto, Michael J.
Earth tales from around the world / by Michael J. Caduto :
illustrated by Adelaide Murphy Tyrol.
p.   cm.
Includes bibliographical references and index.
ISBN 1-55591-968-5 (pbk.)
1. Earth—Folklore.   2. Nature—Folklore.
I. Tyrol, Adelaide Murphy. II. Title.
GR655.I33   1997
398.27—dc21   97-7892
CIP

Printed in the United States of America

0   9   8   7   6   5   4   3   2

Fulcrum Publishing
350 Indiana Street, Suite 350
Golden, Colorado 80401-5093
(800) 992-2908 · (303) 277-1623

To the storytellers
who have kept these tales
alive in our hearts
down through the ages.

To the Roots
that bind us to Earth,
and the branches
that reach for Sun.

Contents

vi

vii

Contents

Acknowledgments

This book, like all that have preceded it, began as an idea that winged into my consciousness and would not fly away until I had written it into life. I owe all to the Creator's fountain of visions, which is ever flowing.

And then, there is this world. I am greatly indebted to Adelaide Murphy Tyrol for the gift of her beautiful, timeless illustrations. Thank you to Suzanne Barchers, children's editor at Fulcrum Publishing; Bob Baron, publisher, and the production staff for lending the support and expertise that helped this vision become a reality. Appreciation goes out to my wife, Marie, who read and commented on the manuscript, and to my parents, Ralph and Esther Caduto, who helped by sharing some stories and translating others. I am grateful to the following people, who also helped with translation: Mimi Emerson, Elaine Georgakopoulos (Greek), Elisheva Kaufman (Hebrew), Raymond and Cecile Levesque (French), Dong Liao (Chinese), Periklis Papadoliopoulos (Greek), Russell Thomas (Portuguese) and Vân Nguyễn MacPherson (Vietnamese). Geoffrey Vitt, Esquire, provided invaluable help with his legal expertise. Finally, I am grateful to all performers, writers and friends who have influenced me and my storytelling over the past two decades since I first told a story to a group of children whose faces were lit by the fireglow.

The mother birds saw the wisdom in Owl's words.

Introduction:
Earth Tells Its Stories

"Now this story, I didn't make it up!" begins a Sefwi storyteller from Ghana.

"Who did then?" asks the audience.

"Once upon a time, in a certain town," says a storyteller from India.

The Mandingo storyteller, who lives in the Gambia River valley of northwestern Africa, begins by saying, "A really unique story has no end."

A popular Arab opening to a story is, *Kan ma kan. Bidaa nihki, willa innam.* "There was, there was not. Shall we tell stories, or sleep on our cots?"

In France, a tale may begin with, *Cric crac, socque, cuiller à pot; marche aujourd'hui, marche demain. À force de marcher; on fait beaucoup de chemin,* which means, "Cric crac, clog, kitchen spoon; walk today, walk tomorrow. By walking and walking, we cover a lot of ground."

Storytellers may cover a lot of ground, but the stories themselves grow from the very Earth upon which they are first told. That is where they take root. Traditionally, the Wolof people from Gambia only tell their stories in the lands where the baobab tree grows. From Siberia to the tip of South America, and from Africa to Polynesia, these stories grew. Through these tales, the natural world speaks to the people who walk upon it and who use it to stay alive. But stories have wings, too, which carry them far and wide on the winds of our imaginations.

The stories in *Earth Tales from Around the World* contain the wisdom that countless generations have harvested by living close to the land, growing their own food and making the things they needed with their own hands. In order to live, they had to take care of the soil, the water, the plants and the animals. As these stories show, people quickly learned that the harm they caused the world around them would one day come knocking on their own door. The care they showed would be returned in kind with food, clean air and water, and materials with which to fashion tools and other necessities. These tales also reveal that life is not all work—the traditional peoples of the world have always enjoyed a beautiful sunset, the sweet smell of a flower and the joy of a newborn fawn.

In many of these stories it is clear that traditional cultures often believe that all of nature is alive: those things that move, and even those that do not. There is a breath of life in a tree, a hawk and the long wind that blows across open places and gently bends blades of grass. A spirit lives in the shadow that grows between the hills as the sun sets, in the rocks of the hills themselves and in the moon that rises into the starry sky. Over and over in these tales we read of the common faith in a benevolent, unseen Creator of the wonders that surround us.

No matter what culture, or cultures, our ancestors come from, the stories in this book can help us trace our roots back to their source. We all have ancestral ties to Native peoples who lived close to Earth. Their wisdom lies deep in our memories. One common thread that runs through these stories is the belief that we are a part of nature, and that the community of people and the natural world depends upon a mutual, respectful relationship. Although we cannot help but change the world as we live in it and use its resources to keep us alive, we *can* do everything possible to have a positive impact, to nurture the natural world, to treat it with care and respect.

Let us pick up this thread of wisdom and use it to bind and heal our ties to Earth and to the lives of people around us. The wisdom of these stories is both a link to our past, and a lifeline to the beautiful, healthy Earth we want to leave as a legacy for future generations.

A Time and Place for Stories

In most traditional cultures, stories are told in special places and at certain times. In Ireland, and in many other lands, stories are shared as friends and family gather by the fireside during the long, cold nights of winter. This is true in France; among the Gê and the Caduveo peoples of Brazil; among the Yamana of Tierra del Fuego; among the Yoruba of Nigeria and among the Tlingit of northwestern North America, who gather in large plank houses to hear the old tales. The tales of Greece are often told by lantern light. The Wolof people tell stories both day and night, at home, in the fields, by the wells and in the village. All it takes to bring a story to life, say the Wolof, is two people gathered together. The Maya of Guatemala and Mexico tell stories around the kitchen fire, during common times of work and when attending marriages, baptisms and funerals. In India, stories are often told to make boring or tedious work more bearable. In some Arab cultures, stories are told both summer and winter, but only at night. Palestinian tales are not shared during the summer, but are often told to small gatherings of people related to the storyteller once the day's work is done and everyone has had their evening meal.

Children are present at most storytellings, but there are certain times, such as after the children have gone to sleep, when adults gather to share stories meant for older ears. Sometimes, the tales go on into the early hours of the morning. While stories were once told to audiences made up of friends and relatives, listeners today may come from far and wide to hear the old tales.

Many cultures believe that telling stories at the wrong time or place will cause bad things to happen. In Iraq, it is said, if stories are told during the day, horns will sprout from your head and your gold will turn into iron. The Bantu of southern Africa say that someone once grew long, black horns after telling stories during the daytime. Some other African cultures believe that stories should only be told at night because, if a child tells stories by daylight, his or her parents will die. A custom among many Native American cultures is that stories should only be told after the last autumn thunder and before the waters of spring flow free. If you tell stories at other times of the year, a snake will bite you, or you may freeze to death.

TRADITIONAL STORIES AND STORYTELLERS

Garingani, n'wana wa Garingani, "I am Narrator, daughter of Narrator." So begins a storyteller of the Shangaan people in southeastern Africa. The audience chants back, *Garingani, Garingani!* Traditionally, the *Garingani,* or "Narrator," is a family's grandmother or eldest woman. While telling her story, she may sing, clap, stomp her feet, drum or play a wind instrument. In Japan, India and Palestine, it is often the elder women who carry the old stories. Women are the traditional Arab storytellers.

As you sit around many traditional storytelling circles, however, the voice that carries the tale may be that of a man or a woman, old or young. Men and women share the storytelling in many cultures, including the Maya. In Ireland, women share stories about music and folk beliefs, as well as stories that record family genealogies. Men tend to tell adventure tales. Men tell most of the stories among the Gê Indians, too. Among the Yamana, men tell stories for entertainment and women commonly share stories in smaller gatherings of family and friends.

A good story involves the audience. The Yoruba storyteller from Nigeria often begins with a riddle. During the story, the teller uses drama and song and often plays drums and other traditional instruments. Many African storytellers, and the Kewa tellers of Papua, New Guinea, use songs in their stories, to which audiences respond. In Vanuatu, Melanesia, the Nguna constantly repeat phrases during the story and listeners join in. Many West African storytellers use elaborate makeup to look like animals or other story characters. While telling a tale, they often stop to comment or ask the audience questions.

THE TALES' TAILS

Tales do have tail ends. Traditional tales often close in a particular way. In Polynesia, the Kapingamarangi end their tales with, *Waranga tangata hua,* which means, "Just a tale the people tell." The Marquesan people, of this same region, simply say, "It is concluded." The Shangaan Garingani spits on the ground at the end of her tale to ward off evil spirits. An Assamese storyteller in India finishes with, "We had to send out clothes to the washerman, so we came home." At the close of a traditional story in Corsica, one might hear, *Fola foletta, dite a vostra; a mea è detta,* "Fable, little fable, tell yours; mine is told." Wolof storytellers use many endings to a *leb,* or "tale." She or he may finish with, *Fi la leb dohé tabi ca gec,* "This tale passed here and entered the sea." Another common Wolof ending is, *Bakan bu ko jeka fon tabi ajana,* "Whoever first understands it, will enter heaven." One of my favorite endings is commonly used to complete French folktales from the Languedoc region, "I've been through a little mouse hole; my tale is finished." As is true in many cultures, Yoruban audiences cheer when they are pleased by a well-told story.

WHY STORIES?

You are sitting around a table with members of your family. It is a holiday gathering or perhaps a wedding. Someone asks, "Did I ever tell you about what happened to Grandpa when he was a little boy?" Maybe a child is acting up. She is boasting that her doll is prettier than her friend's doll. Mother takes her aside and says, "Let me tell you what happened when the birds had an argument about whose young birds were the most beautiful." Here is a story that my mother, Esther (Martone) Caduto, learned from her mother, Elvira Martone, who brought it with her from Italy when she came to the United States in 1918. Notice how a blue jay, which is native to North America, not Italy, has winged its way into the story. This is one of the birds my Grandmother saw on the farm where she lived in rural Pennsylvania.

The Most Beautiful Bird

As the warm days of spring arrived, the birds were busy building nests and laying eggs. When the eggs began to hatch, the mother birds became excited.

Mother Robin watched her young grow stronger each day. Soon, the soft down on their breasts changed into bright red feathers. "My babies are the most beautiful," Robin exclaimed. Indeed, they were handsome young birds.

"But look at the brilliant shades of blue in the feathers of my young," argued Blue Jay. "They are more colorful than the sky! Surely, Robin, they are more striking than your nestlings." And who could argue?

Each mother bird, in turn, proclaimed that her young were the most comely. Finally, Mother Crow said, "No, my babies are the fairest of them all! Look at their long, curved beaks and shiny black feathers. Listen to their powerful voices, 'Caw, caw, caw.'"

Throughout the day, the forests and fields echoed with the raucous voices of mother birds arguing over whose young were the most beautiful. As the sun began to set, the wise owl interrupted the din with her booming voice, *Ogni, Cornachè parè pui bella e la sua matre,* which means, "Every Crow baby looks most beautiful to its own mother." Owl continued, "And this is true of every mother's children. Now look around at each different kind of young bird. Is it not true that every one of them is beautiful in its own right?"

After the mother birds considered what Owl had said and saw the wisdom in her words, they stopped arguing over whose baby was the most beautiful. Soon, however, the chatter again grew loud as they disagreed about who fed their young the best food and whose nest was superior to all the others.

❖ ❖ ❖

Stories are the traditional form of teaching those things that today's children learn in school, at the movie theater, on television, from the computer screen, over the radio and in books, newspapers and magazines. Through stories, children experience the life around them in a different way. Stories convey to each new generation the lessons learned over hundreds, even thousands, of years: values of getting along well with each other and of taking care of the natural world.

Besides entertaining us and helping teach moral lessons to both young and old, tales give us a sense of our own cultures and who we are related to. Some groups of stories, such as those from Italy, Greece, Turkey and Israel, seem to have a close kinship. Stories help to explain the natural world around us; they carry on our religious beliefs, our artistic traditions and the particular ways we use language. The jokes, humor and teasing found in many stories help to relieve the tensions that arise from living in close family and community. In this way, stories are a kind of medicine, a way of healing the wounds of life.

IS IT TRUE?

Stories may grow from wakeful experiences or dreams that visit us by night. There are many forms of story. I often refer to them as stories, tales or folktales. They are also called myths, legends, fables, fairy tales and proverbs. While each of these words refers to a different kind of story, that is not the most important thing to remember. Above all else, we need to keep in mind that stories are the heart and soul of many cultures. They tell us who we are and what we believe in. To traditional cultures, stories are sacred. Let us enjoy these stories. Let us also treat them with respect and reverence.

During pauses in my performances, when I have just finished telling a story, young children often ask, "Is that a true story?" To this I answer, and firmly believe, "Different people believe different things. If you believe a story is true, then it is."

HOW I HAVE RETOLD THESE STORIES

I first began performing stories in 1978. I now present to thousands of people of all ages each year. These experiences help me to understand what contemporary audiences relate to. Each story in this book is retold in a completely original version. The descriptions and dialogue are my own. I have, however, kept the traditional substance and spirit of each story as I found it.

In many cases, I have echoed, as much as possible, the style and voice of the original storyteller. I have tried to strike a balance between preserving the tradition of passing these timeless stories to future generations, while giving them a voice that speaks to children living in today's world.

When choosing these 48 stories from among the roughly 8,000 that I read and considered, I used, wherever possible, collections of tales that were gathered directly from the spoken words of traditional storytellers, rather than from previously published books. In this way, I have made certain that these stories are authentic. I have not, however, taken any tales out of oral tradition for the first time.

In addition, the illustrations throughout this book of all plants, animals, people, clothing and natural environments have been thoroughly researched. All details are accurate according to each culture, geographical setting and, where relevant, period of time.

How to Use This Book

The stories in this book are meant to be read and shared. They are grouped in ten sections that explore Earth and our relationship to it—Earth, Sky, Fire, Water, Seasons & Weather, Plants, Animals, Circle of Life, Stewardship and Wisdom. At the end of each section is a one-page discussion of the lessons from each story. Read a story, then look over these lessons. If you want to use these stories and lessons to learn in a more active way, choose a lesson and bring it to life using one of the ideas from the "Activities" section in the back of the book.

For example, read the Syrian story, "Disappearing Flowers," and the Gypsy (Traveller) story, "The Silkies and the Fisherman's Sons," which reveal, among other lessons, how collecting rare flowers and overhunting animals endangers their existence. Learn about some endangered species in your area and make a list of all the ways in which they enrich our lives. Give something back to those species—complete the Circle of Giving and Receiving—by getting involved with activities and organizations that aim to assure their survival. Read the Jewish tale, "The Garden of Wisdom," or the Scandinavian story, "An Elfin Harvest." Write a tale about what you would have done if you were the main character in each of these stories.

Immerse yourself in *Earth Tales from Around the World*. Visit strange, exciting environments, listen to the animals call and enjoy meeting the many wonderful, interesting people who live in distant lands. Linger in the garden, smell the flowers and look at your reflection in the dewdrops that hang from their petals. The deeper your journey takes you, the more you will understand that we are all connected in the great Circle of Life.

One

Earth

Origin of the Ocean

Guajiro
(COLOMBIA AND VENEZUELA)

BACK WHEN THE WORLD WAS YOUNG, there was no ocean. There was a small, thin lake that wound between the hills. One day, a hen pelican flew toward the shore. She landed on the water, then waddled up onto the land. There, she laid a magnificent egg.

Under the heat of the young sun, the first *Guajiro* man was walking along. The sun had painted his skin dark with its heat and light. As he strode the uneven rocks along the shore, he came upon the pelican and her egg.

"What a wonderful egg," he said to Pelican. "Why have you laid it here upon these rocks?"

"I cannot tell you," she replied. "I am the only one who can know the secret contents of this egg. You must promise me that you will leave it alone."

"Very well," said the young man, "it is your egg, after all."

Then, the pelican turned and waddled away.

"Where are you going?" the young man called after the awkward bird.

"I am going to a dance," she replied. "I will be gone for some time."

The young man, too, went on his way.

When the sun rose the next morning, the young man took a walk. He found the pelican's egg exactly where it had been the day before. He looked all around, but could not see the pelican anywhere. Overcome with curiosity, he picked up the egg. "It is much heavier than I thought it would be," he said to himself. He held the egg to his ear. Inside, he heard a low whooshing sound.

"I must see what is inside this egg!" he cried as he raised it over his head. With a great crunching sound, he smashed the egg against the jagged rocks. Instantly, a flood of seawater poured forth from the egg. Higher and higher the water rose around him as he rushed up the slope. By the time the water had stopped rising, the tops of the mountains Ituhor and Jepitz were the only dry lands remaining.

The young Guajiro began to look around the top of Jepitz where he was stranded. He found that Pelican was also on Jepitz. All the other animals, however, were trapped on Ituhor.

Pelican was angry at the young man for breaking her egg. She had trapped the ocean in the egg so that she could have all the fish to herself. Even though

3

Higher and higher the water rose.

she could still catch small fish offshore from Jepitz, she had to work hard to catch them *and* she had to share them with all the other animals.

With time, the young man began to pace back and forth around the top of Jepitz. He needed to move around, but there was no place to go. The world was covered with ocean. In his boredom, he threw boulders out to sea. He was stranded upon Jepitz for so long, and he threw so many boulders, that great piles of rock built up above the water. Eventually, these rocks formed the cliffs and land masses that make up Earth's dry land. That is how the surface of Earth appears to this day.

The Coming of Earth

Cherokee
(UNITED STATES)

IN THE EARLY DAYS, the animals lived in *Galun'lati*, "above." This, the Highest Place, was farther above the world than the Sky Vault. But it had become too crowded. "What can we do?" they asked. "Soon there will not be enough room for all of us to live here. Where shall we go?"

A great distance below, more than seven handbreadths beneath Galunlati, was a world of water.

"We are going to hold a council of all the animals," said Eagle. "It is time to search for another land in which the animals can live." The animals flew, crawled, hopped, slithered, swam and walked to the gathering place. For many days they met and discussed what must be done.

At last, a small voice said, "I would like to search the water for a place to rest." The animals looked over to see who was speaking. It was the voice of *Dayuni'si*, "Beaver's Grandchild," the tiny water beetle.

"Dayunisi will do well," declared Eagle. "She moves quickly and rarely stops to rest."

When Dayunisi reached the world of water, she swam in large, quick circles upon its surface. To the very ends of the world she swam, but there was no land to be found. Finally, she dove to the depths. Deeper and deeper she went until she reached the soft mud at the bottom of the sea. Dayunisi brought mud up to the surface and it began to grow. Bigger and bigger it grew until it formed the large island we now call Earth.

"Look what Dayunisi has done," cried the animals who were watching from Galunlati. "She has created a place where we can live!"

"Now I must go and tie up the corners so it does not sink," said *Ganan'esgi*, "Spider." Gananesgi spun four strong, thick cords. When these cords were long enough, she fastened them to the four corners of Earth to hold it up.

"It is a good home," said the animals. "But how are we going to live there? We cannot walk around on the soft, wet mud. We will sink."

"I will look for a place to begin our new home," said Eagle. Eagle flew down from Galunlati and searched for a dry place on Earth, but the soil was not yet dry. For many days, Eagle circled, veered and dipped in the air above Earth. At last, Eagle began to tire and the tips of his wings touched the soft

Wherever Eagle's wings were lifted from the mud, a range of mountains formed.

mud. Every time his wingtips dipped into the mud, they created a valley. Wherever Eagle's wings were lifted from the mud, a range of mountains formed. These became the mountains and the valleys in the land of the *Aniyunwiya*, the Real People.

At last, Earth was dry, and the animals arrived. "But we cannot see," they said. "It is too dark. Something must be done." Then they placed Sun in the sky. Each day Sun made an arching journey from east to west.

"That is good," said the animals, "but it is too hot. We are going to burn up." This was when Red Crawfish, *Tsiska'gili*, got his name—his shell was singed until it turned red.

Sun was raised up by a handbreadth. "The heat is still too great," said the animals. Sun was lifted over and over again, a handbreadth at a time, until its arch almost touched the Sky Vault, seven handbreadths above Earth. This height is known as *Gulkwa'gine Di'galun'latiyun*, the "Seventh Height." To this day, Sun makes its journey above Earth under the Sky Vault. At night, Sun continues around below Earth until it rises again in the east.

The "seven handbreadths" in this story shows that this number is important to the Aniyunwiya (Ah-nee-yoon´-wi-yah), the "Real People," who are also known as the Tsalagi, or Cherokee. The celestial beginning of the Aniyunwiya is symbolized by a star with seven points. Each of the seven different kinds of wood that burns in the Eternal Fire represents one of the Seven Clans. There are seven sides to the traditional Council House. Seven important festivals are held each year, but the seventh festival is held just once every seven years. The Seven Colors represent the Four Directions and the positive traits of human beings.

The Coming of Earth

The Earthquake Fish

(JAPAN)

*M*UKASHI, *MUKASHI*, LONG, LONG AGO, Earth was created on the back of *Jishin-uwo*, "Earthquake Fish." All of Japan rides on Earthquake Fish, from the base of its tail at *Aomori* in the north, to the top of its head beneath *Kyūshū* in the south. Like a giant catfish, Earthquake Fish has long feelers that twitch when it is disturbed.

If Earthquake Fish is restless, the ground rumbles. When something causes him to be angry, he flaps his tail and swishes his head back and forth. Swells and heaves then move like waves across Earth's surface. Sometimes, Earthquake Fish flops over, belly-up, and turns upright again. Then, the ground splits open, homes are destroyed and many people are killed.

Back in the youthful days of the world, the restless Earthquake Fish was causing much destruction. Mountains fell, rivers flowed into great cracks in the ground and people's homes dropped from sight. Entire villages disappeared.

"We must do something to control Jishin-uwo," said the gods Katori and Kashima. "Earth is not a safe place for people to live."

"We will go to battle with Earthquake Fish," said the two gods. They began their journey to Earth. In time, Katori and Kashima arrived in the province of Hitachi. That was when Kashima took hold of his great sword.

"With this sword I will quiet the powerful Jishin-uwo," he said. "No longer will he ruin and destroy Earth." With these words, Kashima drove the sword so deep into Earth that its tip came out the other side. He left the hilt sticking up above the ground.

"Because I have placed this sword here," said Kashima, "I am the only one who will be able to lift it."

From that day forth, the patient Kashima has kept a close watch on Earthquake Fish. If Jishin-uwo grows restless, if he begins to thrash with his head and tail, Kashima leaps astride his back and rides him. With his hands, Kashima grabs Jishin-uwo's gills. Kashima's feet push down upon the powerful fins.

"Now you will grow still," Kashima commands.

Over the centuries, this great sword changed into stone. It now steadies the ground and keeps the rocks in place. Today it is known as *Kaname ishi*, the

Kashima drove the sword so deep into Earth that its tip came out the other side.

Rock of Kanamé, which means "rivet rock." It holds the layers of Earth together like the rivet that binds the leaves of a fan.

If Earthquake Fish does not stop thrashing about, Kashima raises up the Rock of Kanamé and presses it down hard upon its back. This rock is so massive that even Earthquake Fish is not powerful enough to move under its great weight. Then the ground stops moving. Peace and calm come over the land once again.

> *The Earthquake Fish is straining,*
> *with Kashima on its back.*
> *Kanamé Rock is reigning*
> *Jishin-uwo cannot crack.*

9

Earth Words

(FRANCE)

MANY GENERATIONS AGO, when the waters ran clear and free and the forest stretched as far as the eye could see and the few villages that had been built were many days apart, there lived a race of people of the woods. They found all they needed in the wild places.

In those days, the woods people understood the ways of nature. Earth spoke to them through the roots of ferns. As the black roots curled and reached through the soil, they formed the letters of an ancient language. In order to read the words, however, one had to uncover every letter. But the fern roots were fragile. Whenever someone tried to dig them up, they would break into pieces and become lost in the grains of soil. The people of the woods, who lived closest to Earth, had uncovered this language one letter at a time over countless generations and were the only ones to have discovered the meaning of these ancient words. Some say the message was the secret of happiness. Others say it was the deepest secrets of Earth itself.

Even though the people of the woods thought little of those who lived in houses, who separated themselves from the air, the water and the wind, the sun and the sky, they were curious about them. On some nights, after the sun had set, they sneaked up to peer through the shutters of people's houses to see what they were about. Those were the days before glass windows. Whenever one of the house people caught a glimpse of the people of the woods, the woods folk melted into the darkness, their feet hardly bending a leaf as they fled.

Back then, meals were cooked over an open fire and many people ate together in one large room. Often, several families lived in one house, which was made of rough-hewn boards and covered with a thatch roof.

One night, in a certain house during the evening meal, someone caught a glimpse of one of the men of the woods looking in from the darkness. "Let us play a trick on them," she said, "and try to learn their secrets."

The next night after everyone had finished eating, they went out into the clearing in front of the house. From the depths of the forest, the people of the

The black roots formed the letters of an ancient language.

woods were watching by the dim moonlight that filtered through the leaves. All night long the people who lived in the house sang songs and danced in their wooden clogs. When the sun was about to rise, they went inside. But they left one pair of clogs out in front of the house and tied the laces together in a neat bow.

To the people of the woods, who walked in bare feet, it looked as if those who lived in the house had removed a pair of their odd-shaped feet and left it behind. The wild folk came closer and closer to the house.

In his curiosity, one of the men of the woods slipped the wooden clogs onto his feet. Suddenly, the shoes started to dance. The wild man could not take them off. Faster and faster the clogs moved in a frenzy of steps that exhausted the horrified man.

"Help!" he cried to the others. "I cannot take them off!" But the sun had risen and his family and friends were afraid to enter the clearing for fear of being seen. Violently the shoes leaped and jerked the man's feet around, twisting his legs. He tried to move toward a rock on which the wooden shoes might be shattered, but they sensed his thoughts, pulled in the opposite direction and danced all the faster.

When the man of the woods was too exhausted to take another step, the people walked out of the door of the house and yelled, "Stop, shoes!" The wooden shoes came to a halt and the man collapsed. The people picked up the man of the woods and carried him, screaming and writhing, to a dark corner of their house. They kept him prisoner for many days.

"You can have your freedom as soon as you tell us the secrets of the Earth words spelled out by the roots of the ferns," they told the wood man. No matter how many times they demanded this of him, he would not speak.

Each night, while the people slept under their thatch roof, the wood man's wife came and whispered to him through the cracks in the shutters, "My dear love, tell them anything they ask, but you must never tell them the secrets of the Earth words. That language is meant only for those who learn to understand it from the ferns themselves. It is not for those who would capture and subdue those things that are wild."

After they had held him prisoner for many days, the people of the house said, "No matter what we do, this wild man will not tell us what we want to know." They released the man of the forest. He took the secrets of the ferns with him. Never again did the woods people risk being caught by the people who live in houses.

That is why the secret of the Earth words remains a mystery. Some say that the Earth words can still be read in the roots of ferns, in the flowers of the sage, in those things that spring from moist, dark soil. This lost language still hangs on in the world by the mere thread of a fern root that grows in the forest where the woods folk live, far beyond the reach of those who live in houses.

12

Lessons

See the "Activities" section for ideas on how to explore these lessons.

Origin of the Ocean explores where the ocean first came from and how Earth developed through time, from ocean to land masses. This story reveals the Guajiro beliefs about how Earth formed and changed. Lessons include the importance of curiosity for learning, the consequences of breaking a promise and the importance of sharing with others.

Lessons from **The Coming of Earth** include the origin of Earth, how Earth's surface formed and the nature of the forces that shape the continents that make up Earth's surface. This story also looks at the relationship between Earth and Sun and why Sun travels across the sky each day, from east to west. In this story, the Cherokee explain their beliefs about how Earth formed and changed. Two important numbers—four and seven—appear in the story.

The Earthquake Fish causes us to ask about the structure of Earth's crust and the true reasons why we have earthquakes. It shows the enormous power of earthquakes and the damage they cause. On a local level, this story explains the geography of Japan and the origin of the Rock of Kanamé, or "rivet rock."

Earth Words reminds us that clean air and water were once common before people polluted the natural world, and that we still get everything we need to live from nature. This French folktale reveals some extremely important lessons: that every culture's original people lived close to Nature—knew her secrets and wisdom—and that we all have something to learn from those people who still live close to the natural world. Everyone can learn about Earth's wisdom by observing her carefully. The lives of the people who live in houses show how the things we do to protect ourselves from nature can also separate us from her. Finally, the story teaches about the roots of ferns, which spread using underground stems called *rhizomes*.

13

Two

Sky

Why the Sky Is High

(MANGAIA/POLYNESIA)

MAUI'S' ADVENTURES ARE THE SOURCE OF MYTH AND LEGEND throughout Polynesia, and there are many tales about his confusing origins. In the following story of his birth, he appears as the demigod son of Makea-tutara and Taranga. At other times Maui' is known as the son of a man, Tangaroa. In "Why the Sky Is High," Maui's' father is the demigod Ru, who lives in *Avaiki*, the Underworld.

Makea-tutara and his wife, Taranga, had four sons and a daughter. One day, Taranga approached Makea-tutara and said, "Husband, I am expecting another child." The family rejoiced at the good news.

Sadly, the child was born before his time. In her grief, Taranga strolled by the seashore. She was consoled by the sound of the waves breaking upon the sand. Taranga cut a length of the curls from her long hair. She rolled the child in these curls and gently gave him to the sea.

When the sea beings found the child, which had not yet taken on its form, they protected and cared for it. The child was hidden in long strands of kelp. One day, a violent storm wracked the sea and tore the child from its place of resting. Surrounded in the folds of a jellyfish, the child washed up on the shore. Crabs, flies and other creatures approached the jellyfish as if to devour it.

One of the sea beings, Tama-nui-ki-te-rangi, saw these animals gathering around the jellyfish. "There must be something inside," he thought. Tama'rangi unwrapped the jellyfish, discovered the child within and brought him to life. In time, Tama'rangi became like a father to the growing child.

As Maui', the child, grew into manhood, Tama'rangi taught him the ways of the sea ancestors. On many evenings, as the dancing sparkles of moonlight flickered on the waters, Tama'rangi spoke of the old songs and legends, the games and dances.

Eyes wide with delight, Maui' marveled at the worlds that Tama'rangi brought to life. "Father, can you show me how the dances are done?" Maui' asked.

"Very well, son," replied Tama'rangi, who sang the songs and danced the dances of the old ones.

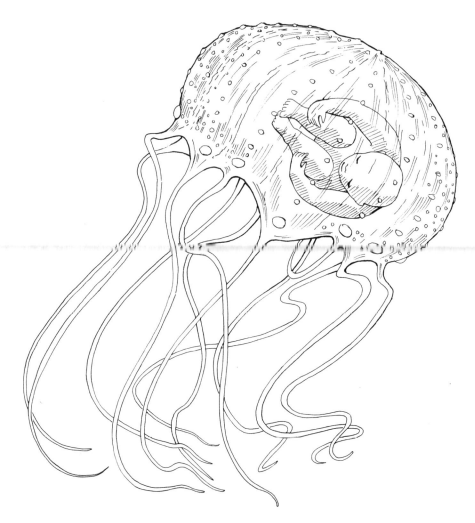

Surrounded in the folds of a jellyfish, the child washed up on the shore.

When the sky was first made, it was fashioned entirely from one vast piece of a beautiful, azure-colored stone. All around on Earth grew the short *teve* trees, barely taller than a full grown human being. Arrowroot was another common plant whose leaves were only half as big as those of the teve trees. Still, the countless green fronds of these plants reached upward and bore the great weight of the stone sky.

In those early days, all the plants, animals and human beings had to survive in the narrow space between Earth and Sky. It was not an easy nor pleasant existence.

"I am so tired of walking with a crick in my neck," someone said.

"If only the sky were higher," another lamented.

"What will we ever do if a fire burns the teve trees and arrowroot?" asked another. "The sky would come crashing down!"

One day, Ru decided to come from the Underworld and visit the beings who lived above. When he found that they were squeezed into such a narrow space, he pitied them.

"I am going to help the creatures who live in this world," he told himself. "There must be a way that the sky can be raised."

Ru searched many days for a means of raising the sky. Finally, he fashioned some long stakes by lashing the trunks of teve trees together. He carried these stakes to the center of the world, *Rangi-motia*, in the middle of the island. Using these stakes, Ru propped up the sky.

Although the sky was not as tall as today, it was much higher than it had been.

"Thanks to the clever Ru!" the people shouted. "He has raised the sky!"

But Maui′ was not impressed. "What are you doing father? Surely you can raise the sky higher than that."

"Did anyone ask you to speak your mind in this way?" Ru demanded of his son.

"No one needs to ask what I think," Maui′ replied. "Besides, I was only trying to help."

Hearing this insolence, Ru became even more angry.

"Keep talking," said Ru. "If you are interested in great heights I will hurl you so high that the world will be a mere speck below you."

"Are these words, or can you really do this thing?" Maui′ challenged.

At that, Ru seized Maui′ and threw him so high that he seemed, for a moment, to disappear. As he began to fall, however, Maui′ grew feathered wings and glided softly to Earth like a bird.

Upon reaching the ground, Maui′ instantly turned back into his original self, but he was much taller than he had been. Taller and taller he grew until his head pressed against Sky. Maui′ the giant then seized both Ru and the sky and threw them so high that they never came down. Ru became entangled in the stars. No matter how hard Ru tried, he could not free himself from the stars overhead.

Some say that Maui′ became the sun.

To this day, Ru's head and shoulders are stuck in the stars. When a piece of his old bones breaks loose, it falls to the earth in a blaze of light as a shooting star. When it lands, it becomes a pumice stone. Many people on the Island of Mangaia still call these stones by their old name, "bones of Ru."

19

Hare Rescues the Sun

Inuit
(Siberia)

AGES AGO, THE *TUNGAKS,* the "Evil Ones," stole the sun from the sky. With no light to guide them, the animals were left to survive on the cold, dark tundra. As they wandered about in lonely blackness, the animals tripped over rocks, bumped into trees and knocked into one another.

"Watch where you're going!" someone would exclaim.

"But I cannot see a thing," would come the reply.

It was hard for the animals to hunt by feeling their way around. Many animals were going hungry. Finally, the animals held a council meeting. All the animals and birds attended so they could have a say in what was to be done to bring back the sun. Raven spoke first.

"Once, the world was lit by the bright warmth of the sun," said Raven as he addressed the animals, "but now we have been left in darkness. The Tungaks took the sun to their hall beneath the Earth, where they keep it in a vessel of crystal white. Someone will have to sneak into their abode and bring back the sun that is rightfully to be shared with all living things. Is there, among you, a being who does not fear the Tungaks, who would venture forth on this great journey?"

"Let us ask Polar Bear," they shouted. "He is the most powerful of us all. The Tungaks could not hurt him."

When Snow Bunting told ancient Owl who was to go, Owl argued against it. "Polar Bear may indeed be powerful," said Owl. "But as soon as he sees something to eat, he will forget that the point of his journey is to bring back the sun."

All the animals nodded in agreement. "Yes, that is Polar Bear," they said.

"Perhaps Wolf should be the one to go," suggested Raven. "He is as strong and swift as the wind."

Owl leaned toward Raven, but her hearing was not very good. "Huh?" she asked Snow Bunting. "What did Raven say?"

"He said that we should send Wolf to bring back the sun."

"That, too, would be foolish," said old Owl. "At the first sight of a rabbit, squirrel or some other food, Wolf would dash off along another trail and be lost to the cause."

"Of course, why could we not see that?" agreed the other animals. "Wolf also follows his stomach wherever it leads him."

"But whom shall we send?" Raven asked the animals.

Off at the edge of the crowd, a small, meek voice could barely be heard. "Why do we not send Hare," said little Mouse. "Could anyone cover the ground faster than Hare once he grabs the sun and escapes from the hall of the Tungaks?"

"Let us send Hare!" cried the other animals.

Snow Bunting leaned over and whispered into Owl's ear. "Mouse says that Hare is fast and will be able to escape from the Tungaks once he grabs the sun."

"Hare is very fast and could outrun any of the Tungaks," said Owl. "And he knows how to focus on getting away better than any other animal. Whhoooo would argue when I say that Hare will bring the sun back safely?"

"Not I," replied each of the animals.

"Then let us listen to Mouse and send Hare to bring back the sun," said Owl.

Raven pointed Hare in the direction of the land of the Tungaks. Hare made the long journey through the endless night before he finally saw a ray of light reaching up into the sky. Carefully, Hare sneaked up to the wall of the great cave of the Tungaks. When he looked inside, he could see that the sun was being held in a magnificent crystal white vessel.

"I must make a plan," thought Hare as he looked around the hall. Sharp, black crystals hung from the ceiling and seemed to grow from the very floor. It appeared that the Tungaks were everywhere, reflected in every crystal lit by the sun. When he looked carefully around the hall, however, Hare saw that there was just one small group of Tungaks who were sleeping comfortably on a bed of reindeer skins on the side farthest from where Hare peered through the crack in the rock.

In one motion that was as quick and fluid as a stream over a waterfall, Hare hopped down through the hole, grabbed the fiery ball of sun from the crystal vessel, thumped the floor of the cave and leapt up through the crack by which he had entered.

"Stop," cried the Tungaks as they fumbled in the darkness. "That fire belongs to us!" But they could not squeeze through the small hole by which Hare had escaped.

By the time the Tungaks found the main door to their hall, Hare was well out ahead of them. But the fiery ball of the sun was heavy. Soon, the Tungaks were close behind and gaining on Hare.

With one great kick, Hare split the ball of the sun's fire in half. Hare kicked again and sent the smaller of the two pieces high up into the sky. This piece became the moon.

Hare Rescues the Sun

Hare kicked the big piece of the fiery ball into the other side of the sky.

Then, with all of his strength, Hare kicked the big piece of the fiery ball into the other side of the sky. As soon as he had done this, a brilliant, warm light shone down on the animals who were waiting on the other side of Earth.

"Look at the sky," they exclaimed, "Hare has brought back the sun!"

Once the Tungaks were out in the light of day, they began to shrink and cower. They could only be near the sun when it was in the crystal white vessel. Quickly, they ran back into the dark cave and were never heard from again.

Ever since Hare's great feat of speed and courage, the animals have gathered in the evening hours when the sun has set and the moon is overhead. At those times they tell the story of how Hare brought back the sun and kicked the moon into the sky. The animals still remember to express their gratitude to the hares for what their ancestor accomplished long ago.

22

First People Make the Stars

Diné /Navajo
(United States)

First Man and First Woman fashioned the discs of Sun and Moon from a great slab of quartz, then decorated them and used lightning to fasten them high in the eastern sky. Then Sun Bearer and Moon Bearer entered the discs and began to move along their paths, guided by the tail feathers of Eagle.

Many chips and pieces of quartz sparkled on the blanket upon which the slab of stone had rested when First Man and First Woman chiseled away the discs of Sun and Moon. Piles of white dust lay about.

"These pieces of stone are beautiful," said First Woman.

"We must make good use of them," First Man agreed.

"Look at the vast empty space still left in the night sky," said First Woman. "These pieces of stone could be used to create patterns of light in the darkness."

Using their stone hammers and chisels to break more pieces of stone, First Man and First Woman then took up their flint knives and carved countless stars. When their work was finished, the blanket was littered with stars and sprinkled with stardust.

"Now," said First Woman, "I am going to arrange these stars in the sky. In these stars I will record the wisdom to guide the human beings. These laws cannot be recorded in the blowing sands or in the changing waters, or they will be altered by the forces of nature. But the People will always be able to look up in the night sky when they are lost and in need of guidance."

First Woman began by creating the star patterns in the sand as a template. While she was drawing, she positioned a strong star in the north.

"This star will be visible to everyone all year long," she explained. "This Campfire of the North will stay in one place. Some will call it the Lodestar, and it will help travelers find their way. There must be a star in each of the four directions, and one in the center." With that, First Woman drew stars in the south, the east and the west. Another star was positioned at the top of the night sky.

Fire Man sent two arrows skyward. These followed a curved path and created a ladder with their trails.

"Be careful, Fire Man," warned First Woman. "Each star must be placed exactly and must follow a certain path." Using a stick, she drew a picture in the

23

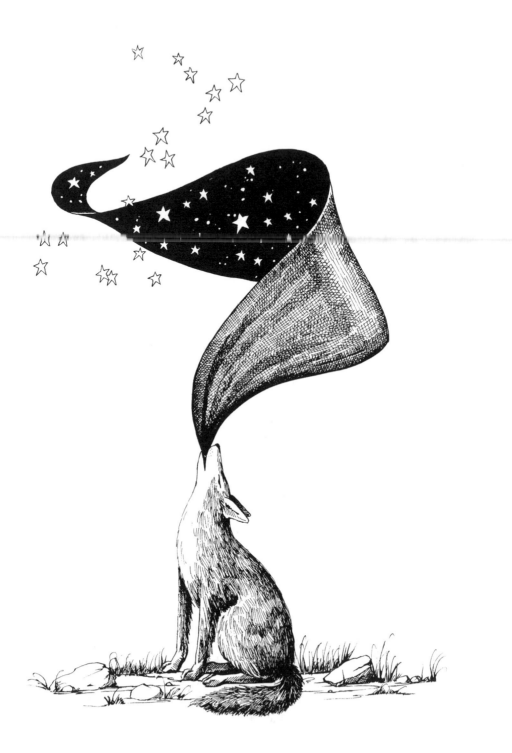

As Coyote swept the blanket over his head, the remaining stardust flew up.

sand that showed Fire Man how the stars should travel through the darkness. Before each star was placed in the sky, First Man fastened a prayer feather to its highest point. Every star was given its own trail to follow, and a special prayer to chant along the way.

Then Fire Man climbed the ladder and placed the North Star in the sky. One at a time, Fire Man placed the larger stars, exactly as First Woman had drawn. First Woman helped by arranging smaller stars in patterns across the sky dome. Coyote, who had been watching from close by, also climbed the ladder and helped place the stars. In this way, they created the constellations.

When most of the larger quartz chips were used up, only tiny fragments and specks of dust remained. With these, First Woman filled Fire Man's hands. He climbed part of the way up the ladder, lit each quartz fragment and speck of dust with a spark of fire, and sprinkled them here and there across the sky, one handful at a time. These clusters of tiny stars symbolize the glowworm and the firefly, or lightning beetle—the living beings of the night that carry a small spark of fire within them.

Before Fire Man came back down to Earth, Coyote grabbed the blanket by a corner. As he swept the blanket over his head, the remaining stardust flew up and formed a glistening band that stretched across the sky. Although some now call this trail the Milky Way, the Diné call it *Yikáísdáhí*. Each star along this path is a footprint of one of the spirits who journeys between Heaven and Earth.

"Now it is done," said First Woman as she looked at the sky. "Someone in each generation will learn the laws of our people as they are recorded in the stars. That person will pass the wisdom down to the next generation so it will be preserved."

First People Make the Stars

The Seven Sisters

Aboriginal
(AUSTRALIA)

IN ONE TRIBE, MANY YEARS AGO, there lived seven girls who had come of age.

"Grandmothers, Grandfathers," they said to the tribal elders, "it is time for us to be tested. We must learn to control our pain, our fear and our hunger. What good will we be if we do not learn how to put our bodies at the service of our minds?"

"It will be a long and difficult journey," replied the elders.

"Yes, we know. But there is no other way."

For the next three years, the girls ate separately from the other members of the tribe. They were given a small meal at sunrise, and again at sunset. Often, they would eat a bit of meat from the emu, the wombat or the kangaroo.

When three years had passed, the elders said, "Come, it is time for you to take a long journey. Are you ready to be tested?"

"Yes, we are ready," replied the girls. All day and night they traveled, swimming and wading great rivers and trekking across hot, sun-streaked plains. As they picked their way through dense brush, thorns cut their skin. Blood trickled from the wounds.

When the girls began to wonder how much farther they would have to travel, one of the elders said, "For the next three suns you will fast as we continue our journey."

Many times the girls felt weak and light-headed, but they continued on. "We will not stop until we have mastered our hunger," they said. After three days had passed, the elders prepared a morning meal of kangaroo. Using a flint knife, each girl cut only a small amount of meat for herself.

"You have done well to control your hunger," said the elders. "Now there are other temptations that you must overcome."

"Tell us what we must do," said the girls. "We will use our wills to pass any test that you present."

"Stand here in a line," said the elders. As the girls stood shoulder-to-shoulder, the elders went up to each and pulled one of their young teeth. Each girl stood and waited her turn. Blood flowed each time a tooth was pulled. After the elders had performed this rite on all seven girls, they asked, "Would you stand here if we came back to pull another tooth?"

The seven young women were lifted up above Earth as a cluster of stars.

27

"You could not make us leave," they replied. "Our wills are stronger than pain." The elders then treated each wound with healing ashes made from the wood of a certain tree.

After a few nights passed and the wounds began to heal, the elders asked "Are you ready for another test?"

"Yes, we are ready," answered the girls.

The Seven Sisters

They led the girls to a new campsite and asked them to spread out their opossum-skin bedding on the soil. At first, the exhausted girls fell fast asleep. Then, something woke them up. They were sleeping near some ant hills and the insects were crawling over their skin. All night long the ants crept across their skin. Even though they were very tired, the girls could not sleep. Still, they did not cry out or complain. When the sun rose at last, the girls went to the elders, smiled and said, "We are ready for the next test."

"We are proud of how you have controlled your hunger and endured the pain," said the elders with a look of satisfaction in their eyes. "You have done well. Now, it is time to test your courage."

"Grandparents, we are ready."

That night, the elders brought the girls to a campsite and told them that the ancestors were buried nearby. In the moonlight, the gnarly arms of ancient trees reached forth as if to capture the girls while they sat by the fire. As they lay falling asleep, the elders told the girls frightening stories about the shape-shifting *muldarpe*, a spirit that can appear as a lizard, a kangaroo or a wombat. All night long the elders spun horrid stories about ghosts and monsters. As the shadows loomed large in the firelight, the moonbeams and the howling wind seemed to be horrible beings come to life. A dingo's blood-chilling cry shattered the night. An owl called as the elders stalked the edge of the clearing dressed as spirits. The girls fought to control the urge to run from that place. They lay still, closed their eyes and said nothing.

In the morning, the elders smiled as they stood before the girls. "You have overcome hunger, pain and fear. Now we will return to our home and have a celebration."

When the people from the neighboring tribes gathered, the girls stepped forward and said, "Sisters, we have come through the long, hard tests of the elders. By forgetting ourselves, we overcame hunger, pain and fear. Only when we leave the self behind, when we escape selfishness and greed, can we then think of others. This is the way to happiness. It is the will of the Great Spirit that you, too, should take this journey." When the other girls heard these words, and witnessed the generosity of spirit among the seven young women, they were eager to follow the path of greatness.

The Great Spirit was deeply satisfied with the courage shown by the seven young women and the example they set for others. He turned to a brilliant star spirit and said, "Go to these young women and raise them into the sky." Without death or suffering, the seven were lifted up above Earth as a cluster of stars. To this day, the Aborigines see the constellation of the Seven Sisters as a reminder of this story and the great deeds of those young women. This constellation, which some know as the Pleiades, is a source of courage and inspiration.

28

A Golden Angel Egg

(CZECHOSLOVAKIA)

BLACKBIRD, STARLING AND TIT were out gathering food for their young. "I must collect as many worms as I can hold," said Blackbird. "My young nestlings are just learning to fly, and they need all the help they can get."

"You have a lot of work ahead of you," said Tit. "It takes much patience to teach the young ones how to use their wings properly. It is easy for us adults to forget what it was like when we were learning how to fly for the first time."

Starling was listening from her perch up in the birch tree. "Did you know that, at one time, even adult birds did not know how to fly?"

"How could that be?" asked Blackbird. "The power of flight has always been passed down from one generation to the next."

"True," replied Starling, "but I can tell that you have never heard the story of how birds first learned to fly."

"I would love to hear that story!" said Tit excitedly.

"I first heard the story from Raven. He told it to me last winter when the snow was deep. He said that his grandfather told it to him. His grandfather heard the story from his great-grandmother, and it has been in the family as far back as anyone can tell."

"Then it must be a true story," said Blackbird.

"Of course," said Starling. "Once the sun sets and you can see stars in the sky, it sometimes looks like a star comes shooting down in a bright streak of light."

"Yes, I have seen that!" cried Tit.

"Me, too," said Blackbird.

"Exactly," said Starling, "we all have. Which proves the story is indeed true.

"But, says Raven, some of those lights that we think are falling stars, well, they are nothing of the kind."

"What are they?" asked Tit impatiently. "Tell us what they are."

"Some of them are really golden angel eggs that have rolled out of their nests and fallen from the heavens. On the way down, they grow hotter and hotter. Then they begin to glow as if they are on fire."

Blackbird interrupted, "I have heard people call them meteors."

"Yes, those are the ones," said Starling as she nodded in agreement.

"One evening, just as the birds were getting ready to sleep, one of those star lights shot across the sky. It was a brighter falling star than anyone had ever seen before. It landed not far from where the birds were roosting."

29

A baby angel hatched in front of all the birds.

"What did they do?" asked Tit, who could not contain her curiosity.

"They walked, swam and hopped toward the place where the thing landed."

"Why didn't they … ?" Tit started to ask.

"Because birds could not yet fly!" interrupted Starling a bit peevishly. "So it took the birds a long time to reach the landing spot. When they got there, they found a golden, glowing egg half buried in the ground. Stork reached the egg first because her legs were the longest, and she traveled faster than any other bird. Stork found that the egg was very hot. When she bent over to investigate, the feathers on her head were burned off. Storks still have no head feathers."

"So the birds waited for the angel's egg to cool down?" asked Blackbird.

"No, they were afraid that, if it cooled off, the chick inside that egg would die. Stork picked it up with her feet and waddled over to the other birds to show them what she had found. But her feet were so badly burned that she jumped right into the lake to soothe them. Raven says that is why storks are still wading around in the shallow water."

By now, several other birds had flown in to listen to the story. "What happened next?" asked Swallow.

"Goose waddled over to the egg and sat down upon it to brood the chick inside. All the other birds watched as smoke began to rise from under Goose's breast. When she could endure the heat no longer, she ran down to the lake and cooled off by swimming around with her breast completely underwater. Geese are still swimming around like that, cooling off their breasts.

"Each different kind of bird in turn brooded that egg to hatch it," Starling explained.

"Even the swallow?" asked Swallow.

"Yes, the swallow did, too," replied Starling. "The only bird who did not care enough to try to hatch the chick inside that golden angel egg was Hen. 'I don't have time to hatch strange eggs,' Hen said. 'I have all I can do to scratch and sift through the dirt looking for something to feed me and my family.'"

"That Hen, if she were here right now I would tell her how selfish she was being," said Tit indignantly.

Starling looked over at Tit, shook her head, and continued. "When the very last bird was sitting upon the angel's egg ... ."

"And who was that?" asked Blackbird.

"It was Wren, if you must know," said Starling. "Now may I continue?"

"Yes, yes, go on," said Hawk, who had flown in a while ago. "Now please, everyone, listen to Starling. Let her finish."

"Well, that egg began to shake and crack," said Starling. "Then, a baby angel hatched in front of all the birds. It spread its wings and began to fly up toward the heavens."

"You have all been so kind," the angel said to the birds as it flew overhead. "Without your help, I would have never hatched. I am going to repay your generosity with the gift of flight. See how I flap my wings and take to the air? All of the birds who helped me to hatch are now able to fly."

"How do we begin?" asked the birds.

"Simply flap your wings as I am doing," replied the angel. "Let's try it together—flap ... flap ... flap ... and up you go!"

With that, all the birds took to the air for the very first time. The sky was filled with flapping wings, colorful feathers and joyful songs.

"But, but what about Hen?" asked Tit.

"Because she refused to brood the angel's egg, she did not receive the gift of flight," said Starling.

Now that the story was over, the birds remembered they had work to do. They flew up into the air, sang their songs, thanked Starling and went off in all directions. At last, Starling was alone, perched in the birch tree. She looked down and saw Hen pecking at the ground as she walked along. Hen had a long journey home.

A Golden Angel Egg

Lessons

See the "Activities" section for ideas on how to explore these lessons.

Why the Sky Is High reveals beliefs of the people of Mangaia/Polynesia about the nature and color of the sky. This story looks at the origin of the sun. It explores the source of meteors or "shooting stars" and what they are made of. In this tale, we learn the origin of Maui', of how he was cared for by the sea beings and then adopted by Tama'rangi.

Hare Rescues the Sun looks at the origin of the sun, how the sun creates heat and light, the origin of the moon and where moonlight comes from. You can also use this Inuit story to begin exploring how our eyes detect light. Other lessons include that each animal has its own particular character and habits— some animals are active by day *(diurnal)*, others are active at night *(nocturnal)*.

The Diné (Navajo) story **First People Make the Stars** looks at how stars were formed, where the Milky Way came from and why we see patterns of stars, *constellations,* in the night sky. These star images inspire stories by which wisdom is recorded. As in many cultures, this story shows how the Diné use the North Star to find their way. We learn why stars possess the nature and color of the mineral called quartz. The number four is important in this story. Other lessons explore the source of light in fireflies, or lightning beetles, and their larvae, called glowworms. Fireflies are also a part of the Japanese story, "Princess Firefly's Lovers," in the next section.

The Seven Sisters introduces the origin of the constellation, the Seven Sisters, which is also known as the Pleiades. This constellation is a source of courage and inspiration. This story teaches about the Aboriginal rite of passage from a girl to a young woman. It shows that we must learn to control hunger, pain and fear in order to discipline mind and body. This is how we escape selfishness and greed in order to be generous and to think of others. The number seven is significant in this story.

A Golden Angel Egg discusses the origin of meteors or "shooting stars." This Czechoslovakian story explores how birds learn to fly, why Stork, Goose and Hen appear and act as they do and how eggs are brooded and hatched. We learn the importance of, and the rewards that come from, helping a group achieve a common goal.

32

Three

Fire

The Coming of Fire

Aboriginal
(AUSTRALIA)

GOORDA, THE FIRE SPIRIT, lived alone among the stars of the Southern Cross. He was a great hunter who traveled between three different campfires, known as the Pointers. When he was lonely, Goorda wanted his neighbors to visit.

"Would you like to come to my camp?" he asked. "I will give you as much as you can eat, and we can share songs and stories."

Goorda prepared his camp. He watched and hoped that the visitors would come, but no one arrived. Down below, on Earth, Goorda saw that people lived together. They helped each other hunt and gather roots and nuts. Children swam and played games with their friends. Adults told stories when they gathered in the evening. "Come," Goorda called down to Earth, "there is much game where I live. You may hunt here." But Earth's people did not come.

One night, Goorda saw the Earth people eating raw meat from the kangaroo and the goanna lizard. He watched them sit close together in order to keep warm as they ate. "Fire, that is what the Earth people do not have," he said to himself. "But fire is something I have enough of for everyone. I will bring it to the Earth people."

"Please take me with you!" Goorda cried to one of the falling stars as it streaked toward Earth. But it did not stop. After he banked his fires so they would not go out, Goorda followed the path of the falling star and shot toward Earth in a bright flash. He headed for the shore opposite where a group of people were gathered along the banks of the Gainmaui River by Caledon Bay.

"I come bearing a gift for you," said Goorda. When his feet touched ground, however, the brush began to crackle with flames. Soon, a blaze was roaring along the riverbank. Across the river, the people picked up their spears and watched, their faces kissed by the red hues of the dancing flames. When the heat from the fire became so great they could feel its pain, they screamed and fled from Goorda.

"Stay! Do not go!" Goorda cried, "I will not hurt you." But flames spread everywhere he walked. Those people who jumped into their canoes and paddled away from shore survived. A goanna lizard burrowed into the ground and closed its doorway with soil. It, too, escaped the smoke and flames. Nearby,

The spider, Garwuli, survived by taking refuge in the deep fissure of a broken rock.

the spider, Garwuli, survived by taking refuge in the deep fissure of a broken rock. A cloud of honeybees rose into the air and fled to the shelter of a hollow tree a great distance away. The swifts circled overhead and caught insects that fled upward from the flames. Crocodiles, barramundi fish and other water creatures swam away from the hot, steaming waters along the riverbank. All of these escaped Goorda's fire.

But Goorda, not understanding, tried to get close to people so he could visit with them. Some people were burned in their huts. Others fled in terror. By the end of the day, Goorda looked out over a silent, black, smoldering land. Overhead, a red-winged parrot called and circled in search of a place to land, then flew away searching for safety until it sank down below the horizon in the distance.

Exhausted, Goorda sat down to rest. He found a kangaroo that had been burned and began to eat. "This will not do," he said. "I will have to appear to the Earth people in a different way, or they will always flee from me." Goorda changed to the form of a person and painted a diamond on his breast. "This will be my symbol," he said. "Now I am ready to greet people and teach them how to use fire in a good way."

When the sun rose over the blackened land Goorda had created, a curious group of hunters came wandering. Goorda saw them and stood up. "Hello, my friends," he said. Flames began to shoot from the end of the stick he held in his hand. "Do not fear," said Goorda. "Fire can be of use to you. It can cook your food." Saying that, Goorda picked up a piece of blackened kangaroo, took a bite and chewed. "See, it tastes much better this way."

Goorda handed the meat to the men and each carefully took a bite as they passed it around. "Indeed, it is very good," they agreed. They searched around for more meat and ate their fill. As they were eating, Goorda showed them the ways of fire. He demonstrated how to create fire by holding a stick between the hands and turning it quickly while the end sits in a small hole bored into another piece of wood. In a short time, the light of an ember appeared where the two sticks met. "Be careful with flame," said Goorda. "Clear the brush away from your campfires and watch the flames closely so they do not spread.

"When the leaves and branches are dry, you can light a fire to herd the animals so hunting will be easier. Later, when the rains come and the Moon Man has once gone and returned, those trees and bushes will sprout new leaves and twigs for the wallaby and kangaroo to eat."

The hunters learned everything Goorda had to teach, then they thanked him and walked back to tell their families. Satisfied with his visit, Goorda again took on the form of the Fire Spirit. He streaked up through the icy blackness toward his home in the Southern Cross. The flames of his fires continue to dance and flicker in the night skies.

37

The Coming of Fire

Hippo Befriends Fire

Krobo
(GHANA)

HIPPO ONCE HAD A HANDSOME COAT OF FUR. His fur was long and soft to the touch. Hippo was so proud of his fur that he spent many hours looking at his reflection in the slow waters at the river bend. He used a fishbone comb to keep his fur neat and shiny.

"Don't you think my fur is the thickest of all the animals?" he used to ask his friend Rat.

"Yes, yes, of course," Rat would answer. Hippo was Rat's friend, after all, and was a kind-hearted animal who treated Rat well.

Back in those days, Hippo lived on land in a large grass house. Rat and Hippo spent many days together. One day, Hippo visited Rat, and they played a game of tag. Hippo was very careful when playing with Rat because he was so much larger than his friend. On this day, however, Hippo slipped and accidentally stepped on Rat's tail.

"Ow!" she screamed. "You should watch where your big feet are going!"

"I am very sorry," Hippo said to his friend. "I did not mean to step on your tail. Please do not be angry."

But it was no use, Rat was convinced that Hippo had stepped on her tail on purpose. A few days later, Rat was talking to Hippo when she said, "Did you know that Fire is one of my best friends? Have you ever met Fire?"

"Yes, we have met," said Hippo. "But I do not know Fire very well."

"I am a closer friend with Fire than you are, Hippo. Would you like to become better acquainted with Fire?"

"Yes I would," said Hippo excitedly. "But where does Fire live?"

Rat gave Hippo directions to Fire's house. Hippo, who was jealous of Rat's friendship with Fire, left right away to visit Fire so that they, too, could be close friends. When Hippo approached the home of Fire, he saw how bright Fire was and felt the heat of his flames. Hippo kept his distance.

"Fire," said Hippo, "I think it's time that we should become closer friends. Will you please accept my invitation to visit me in my home for dinner?"

"Why do you want me to visit your home?" asked Fire. "You and I are already friends, and I am not sure that you would want me to come to your grass house. If you are like so many of the other animals, you would flee before I even entered the doorway. I have visited the birds, and they have flown away.

Hippo saw how bright Fire was and felt the heat of his flames.

The snakes, the human beings and even the lions run when I approach. For this reason, I stopped paying visits to my friends long ago."

"I would not run," Hippo exclaimed. "I am not afraid of you, Fire. Won't you please be my guest? Please!" implored Hippo.

"All right, enough already," Fire said at last. "When would you like me to visit?"

"How about tomorrow?" asked Hippo. "I will prepare a nice meal and we can play some games."

"That would be fine," said Fire. "I will arrive in the evening."

Hippo was so excited that he went straight home and began to prepare for Fire's visit. He slept lightly and arose with the sun. That morning, just to be sure Fire had not forgotten, Hippo stopped at Fire's house to remind him about the visit.

"Yes, yes, I will be there!" said Fire.

As the day wore on, Hippo put the finishing touches on the dinner and straightened up around his grass house. He wanted everything to be just right for Fire's visit.

When the sun began to set, Hippo heard strange noises outside. He stepped out the door of his house and saw birds flying and screeching in terror from the nearby trees. All of his neighbors seemed to be running past him as fast as they could go.

But Hippo waited patiently for his friend to arrive for dinner. Hippo saw a bright, red light approaching in the distance, but he did not move. He grew hotter and hotter, but still he stood in his doorway. At last, his fur caught fire and his grass house began to burn. Hippo was terrified! He ran down to the river and threw himself into the deep water.

Hippo's house was reduced to a pile of ashes, and he had nowhere else to live on land. His fur was completely burned away. From that day forth, Hippo was no longer proud of his appearance. Ever since, he has spent most of his time hiding in the deep waters of the river. Anyone who has met Hippo down by the river knows that he is no longer the kind, gentle soul that he once was,

40

Pele's Wrath of Fire

(Hawaii)

Dancers flowed to the rhythm of the drums while a procession of people in brightly colored costumes moved past the feast offering of fish, fowl and pigs. Wrestlers, racers and other challengers met in contest while, nearby, musicians played for the hula dancers. In Puna, on the island of Hawaii, it was the time of the festival of Lono makua.

The local chief, Kahawali, challenged his friend, Ahua, to a contest down the slope of Ka holua ana o Kahawali. Each would slide down the slope on a sled called a *holua*. Ahua went first and had a strong run. Then Kahawali grasped his holua, ran to full speed and plunged down the slope with the holua beneath him. Kahawali went farther and won the contest.

As Kahawali finished his winning run, cheering voices rang out and echoed amid the hills. Up in the fiery crater of the volcano Kilauea, the goddess Pele heard the celebration and became excited. She took the form of a woman and left Kilauea to join in the festivities.

"What is the excitement about?" Pele asked the people in the crowd.

"Did you not see the magnificent run that Kahawali made on his holua?" they asked Pele. "There is no one who could beat him!"

"Hmm," Pele thought to herself, "no mere human could better me at the holua contest."

Even though it was not customary for a woman to enter this particular sport, Pele cried out, "Chief Kahawali, I wish to challenge you to a contest upon the holua."

"Very well," replied Kahawali, who also saw Pele as a woman, "but be prepared to lose!"

Pele and Kahawali oiled up the runners of their holuas. Soon, they were streaking down the slope. Kahawali was the most experienced of the two sledders and his sled traveled the longest distance.

"Your sled is superior to mine," Pele insisted. "Let us switch sleds and try again."

"*Aole!*" cried Kahawali, "No! Perhaps my wife could use my holua, but you are a stranger. Who are you to ask?" With those words, Kahawali lunged and flew farther down the slope upon his sled.

Kahawali used his long spear to create a bridge upon which he crossed.

Oh, but Pele was angry. With stomping feet she took her natural form and split the mountain in two. People fled in terror as the earth quaked. Pele screamed, "Speak Kilauea." There was a deep rumbling, then tongues of fire and rivers of glowing lava flowed from the volcano. Pele called thunder and lightning down from the sky and rode the burning floes down the slope toward Kahawali, consuming everyone and everything in her path.

When Kahawali turned and saw that Pele was almost upon him, he grabbed his spear and ran. The flaming mass advanced with great speed. Kahawali came to his mother's house. They rubbed noses in a compassionate greeting. Kahawali said, "My heart goes out to you, but your time is at hand."

Next, Kahawali arrived at the door of his own house, where his wife and two children, Poupoulu and Kaohe, waited. He rubbed noses with the three and said, "Pele is nearly upon us!"

"Please, do not go," his wife implored. "Stay here with us. What happens to one, will happen to us all."

"There is a great hole in my heart," said Kahawali with tears in his eyes, "but I must go." He ran on with the lava close behind. In a short distance, the trail came to a deep chasm that was too wide to be jumped. Kahawali used his long spear to create a bridge upon which he crossed. As soon as he came to the other side, Kahawali grabbed the spear and ran onward. The lava poured into the chasm behind him, filled it and continued the chase.

Just as Kahawali reached the ocean, his brother was returning from a fishing trip. Kahawali jumped into the canoe and the two of them paddled furiously away from the island. When Pele saw they were escaping, her rage grew into fury. She threw flaming rocks from Kilauea at the brothers, which landed harmlessly in the sea and created boiling rolls of steam. Pele blew her deadly, sulfurous smoke and smothering ash in their direction, but the wind carried it back in her face.

When Kahawali and his brother were a safe distance out to sea, he used his spear for a mast and his royal cloak for a sail. The sail caught a wind from the east, which carried the brothers to safety on the island of Maui. In time, they journeyed to Molokai, and then on to Oahu, the home of their father, Kolonohailaau, and sister, Kane wahine keaho. Kahawali and his brother settled on the island of Oahu with their father and sister.

It is said that Pele is still angry at Kahawali. At some time in the future, she will again unleash a rage of fiery destruction. No one knows when that time will come.

Princess Firefly's Lovers

(Japan)

On a night during the seventh month, as the moon arched across the evening sky, a gentle wind rocked the crimson petals of a lotus that floated upon the marsh. Cradled within this beautiful bloom sat Hotaru, Princess of the Fireflies. Her gentle, golden light was a star blazing on a dark sky of water.

Now that she had come of age, Hotaru was allowed to fly among the lotus petals, past the wildflower meadows and out over the rich rice fields. Wherever she flew, hundreds of suitors followed. Hotaru's light worked its spell. Many were struck by her beauty. Passion filled their hearts. They were helpless before her brilliance.

At last, Princess Hotaru came to rest on the petals of her lotus bloom.

"Please," cried each of the suitors that landed on the flowers and lotus leaves surrounding Hotaru, "take me for your husband."

"One alone shall win my heart," she replied.

"What must we do?" they asked.

"Whoever will become my husband must bring me a gift of fire," she declared. "You must show that you love me more than life itself."

"My lady, this I will gladly do," said Golden Beetle.

"I will not return unless I capture your gift of fire," declared Hawkmoth.

"Neither of you can fly as swift as I," boasted Scarlet Dragonfly. "I will bear Hotaru's fire upon my wings before either of you have reached a circle of light."

Off into the night flew the three suitors, as quickly as their wings could carry them. Scarlet Dragonfly was the first to see a flame flickering in the darkness ahead. Dragonfly hovered outside the open window of a young girl. She sat at her desk and read a love letter by candlelight. Tears slid down her cheek and splattered onto the parchment. Dragonfly flew bravely toward the flame so that he might snatch a bit of fire for Hotaru. Instantly, his wings were singed. "Oh, how sad!" cried the girl, "why have you flown into the fire?" Scarlet Dragonfly lay silent and lifeless upon the desktop.

Buzzing through the soft night air, Golden Beetle came to a house in which a fireplace was lit. Inside, a woman sat mending some clothes by the firelight

Cradled within a beautiful lotus bloom sat Hotaru, Princess of the Fireflies.

while her husband carved a wooden spoon with his knife. Golden Beetle whirred past the woman's left ear, causing her to jump. Instantly, there came a crackling and a small flash in the fireplace. A puff of smoke rose up with the sparks.

"Whatever could that have been?" asked the woman. She rose from her chair and found the toasted beetle upon the hot coals. "Look, Dear," she said, puzzled, "this beetle threw itself into the flames and died."

In time, Hawkmoth fluttered toward a house from which light shown through the paper windows. He flew into a room where a student sat reading by the light of an oil lamp. Hawkmoth fluttered closer and closer to the flame as the student tried to brush him away. At last, Hawkmoth plunged into the candlelight in his attempt to capture fire for his lover. Hawkmoth singed his wings and fell into the pool of lamp oil. As Hawkmoth struggled to escape, he was engulfed in the thick oil and drowned.

Princess Firefly's Lovers

Meanwhile, Hotaru sat safely within the petals of her lotus bloom. As she gazed up at the stars, waiting for her suitors to return, a golden light streaked across the sky. "It must be a falling star!" she thought. Closer and closer came the light, until Hi-Maro, Prince of the Fireflies, perched upon a petal at the edge of Princess Hotaru's lotus. Hi-Maro unfolded his wings to reveal the brilliant flame of life within. Hotaru leapt with joy at the sight of the Prince's fire.

"I have come to ask you to be my wife," said Prince Hi-Maro. He flew up over the marsh and put on a wondrous display of golden, dancing starlight that captured Hotaru's heart. The Prince and Princess were wed later that night. Generations of fireflies have lived amid the lotus petals ever since.

While Hi-Maro wooed his lover by the light of the moon, the tragedy of Hotaru's suitors continued. One after another, they threw themselves into flames in vain attempts to capture the fire of Hotaru's desire. They visited tall candles in Buddhist temples, lamps in the courtyards of shrines, kitchen lanterns and sparks streaking from chimney tops. By morning the bodies of Hotaru's suitors lay thick across the land.

To this day, during the time of the seventh moon, Princess Hotaru's suitors fly through the darkness on their quest for the fire that will win her heart. Each morning, people find the places of night-fire littered with bodies. "Look," they say, "many lovers tried to win the heart of Princess Firefly last night."

46

Lessons

See the "Activities" section for ideas on how to explore these lessons.

The Coming of Fire is a powerful story explaining the Aboriginal belief that fire first came from among the stars of the Southern Cross. This tale shows the immensely destructive power of fire. It also describes many ways that fire can be useful to people and tells how fire can be created.

Hippo Befriends Fire is a bittersweet Krobo story about the once kind-hearted Hippo who does not understand how destructive Fire can be. Because of his insecurity, stubbornness and jealousy over Rat's supposed friendship with fire, Hippo nearly gets himself killed. Hippo's long, soft coat of fur is burned away and he becomes forever bitter. Rat's anger and mistrust lead her to act in a way that nearly kills her close friend, Hippo.

In **Pele's Wrath of Fire,** we learn of native Hawaiians' great fear of the fire that comes from within Earth. This story looks at the mythical cause of volcanic eruptions and earthquakes. It describes the nature of an eruption, including lava flow and the violent release of hot rocks, ash, steam and sulfurous smoke. In the story, a volcanic eruption is caused by goddess Pele's rage, which can flare up at any time. Pele is also the cause of lightning and thunder. Finally, we learn of Hawaiians' love of races, other contests and celebrations.

Princess Firefly's Lovers is a sorrowful Japanese tale that explains how fireflies court with a beautiful exchange of light. This story makes a connection between fireflies and the wet places where lotus flowers bloom. We learn why many different kinds of insects are attracted to lights at night, even though they are often destroyed. Read the Diné (Navajo) story, "First People Make the Stars," which also speaks of fireflies.

47

Four

Water

Natsilane & the Killer Whales

Tlingit
(Canada and United States)

Natsilane (Noht-sy-cla´-nay) was a great hunter. Whenever he went out in his dugout canoe he always remembered that the sea lions he was about to hunt were a gift from the Creator. He hunted with respect and reverence for the gift of these powerful animals. In return, the Chief of the Sea Lions respected Natsilane.

But the oldest among Natsilane's three brothers-in-law was jealous of his success. "We must do something about Natsilane," he said. "He always jumps great distances from the canoe onto the rocks when we are hunting sea lions. I think he is trying to make us look bad."

"No," said the two younger boys, who had grown to respect Natsilane, "he just wants to prove himself to us and the other people in the village."

"We'll see," said the oldest brother-in-law with a dark look in his eye.

The next day, Natsilane and his brothers-in-law paddled their dugout canoe in search of sea lions. They journeyed out to one of the islands far away from the coast. As the four young men paddled near the island, Natsilane leaped from the canoe and speared a sea lion.

"Well done Natsilane," said the oldest brother-in-law. "You are such a great hunter that you do not need us!" At that, he paddled the canoe away from the island.

"Where are you going?" asked the younger boys. "We cannot leave Natsilane alone!"

"Don't worry," said the oldest. "We will come back to get him once he has learned his lesson." But he planned to leave Natsilane alone on the island for good.

Natsilane sat down on the rocks and watched the canoe grow smaller until it disappeared in the distance. The sound of the wind and the waves breaking on the rocks lulled him to sleep. As he slept, the Chief of the Sea Lions visited him. "You will come to live with us," he said. "We will take care of you as we would one of our own."

The sea lions befriended Natsilane, and he soon found himself in a strange land beneath the ocean. He dwelt in a house made of abalone shell. The bluish light that surrounded him filtered through windows made of mother-of-pearl.

All during that summer, Natsilane lived in the house of the sea lions. As long as he was inside, he could breathe. But, whenever he went through the door, he had to hold his breath as he used to do when he was diving from the shore. On his brief journeys from the abalone house, Natsilane foraged along the rocky bottom for crabs, sea cucumbers and other things to eat. Whenever he was very hungry, the sea lions brought him salmon and other good foods.

But Natsilane became homesick. He dreamed of the smell of cedar as he walked through the forest. "The leaves are beginning to glow with the fires of autumn," he thought. "Now the berries are ready to be eaten and the incense will burn upon the hearth of the evening fires."

Natsilane spoke to the sea lion chief. "Please, allow me to return to my people."

"You may begin your journey home under one condition."

"Whatever you say," Natsilane agreed.

"The whale is an enemy who hunts us without remorse. You must create an animal who will kill the whale."

"This I will do," replied Natsilane.

The chief of the sea lions left Natsilane. When he returned, he was carrying two stomachs from the seals. "Blow into these and they will carry you up to the surface." Natsilane inflated the two bladders and tied them around his chest. He took a deep breath, stepped out of his abalone house and floated quickly to the surface. Soon he was riding upon the waves as the sea lions towed him to the mainland.

When Natsilane stepped upon the sandy shore, he thanked the sea lions for all they had done. "Goodbye, my friends!" He waved as they swam away.

Secretly, Natsilane visited his wife and obtained his carving tools. He went back to the shore and set up camp. First, he dug four large pools near the shore. Then he fashioned the first whale killer from a spruce log, carving sleek, powerful jaws set with rows of sharp teeth. Natsilane created an arched fin upon its back, a blowhole and a long, sculpted tail with a wide fluke. He used ashes to blacken the back and sides, but left the belly white. When the whale killer was complete, Natsilane placed it in the first pool. It floated for a short while, then sank.

Next, Natsilane carved a whale killer from the wood of the hemlock. When he placed this one in the first pool, it circled several times, jumped into the second pool, then it, too, sank. "This will not do," thought Natsilane. After searching for some time, he found a beautiful tree of the red cedar. From its trunk he carved another whale killer. This whale killer circled in the first pool, leaped to the second, circled and then leaped to the third pool, where it came to rest on the bottom.

52

The fourth whale killer made a great arching leap into the ocean.

Now Natsilane's carving skills had grown. From yellow cedar he carved a fourth whale killer that outshined the rest and was the largest of all. As he carved, Natsilane sang the ancestral songs. This magnificent creation circled in each of the pools and lept from one to the other until it reached the fourth pool. After circling four times, it made a great arching leap into the ocean. From there it sang a song to the other animals who still lay in their pools. When they heard this call, the three rose from the bottom, bounded from pool to pool and then out to sea.

"This powerful animal I will call Whale Killer," said Natsilane, "for he will be able to dive deep into the sea. The spruce-wood creature will be Porpoise. Blackfish will be the name of the creature made from hemlock. The leaper made from red cedar, who likes to play, will be Dolphin."

53

Natsilane & the Killer Whales

When Natsilane heard that his brothers-in-law were out canoeing to hunt sea lions, he remembered what the oldest among them had done to him. Natsilane set Whale Killer upon them. "But bring back the two young boys," he said. "It is the older one who has done me harm."

Whale Killer found the canoe of Natsilane's brothers-in-law. It swam up from below and capsized the canoe. As the three were drowning, Whale Killer swam beneath the two younger boys and said, "Ride on my back, and I will bring you to shore." Whale Killer carried the two boys to a reef. From there the sea lions took them to the abalone house beneath the sea.

That night Natsilane did not sleep. He feared that the young boys had been killed because of his desire for vengeance. The sun rose over Natsilane pacing upon the sand. He looked up and saw a seagull circling overhead. "Your two young brothers-in-law have been saved," it said. "But you must keep your promise to the sea lions before they will be returned to you."

Immediately, Natsilane remembered what he had made the great animal for. He summoned Whale Killer. "You will not kill men!" cried Natsilane. "You are made to protect the sea lions from their enemy, the whale. Go now and fulfill my promise." As soon as Whale Killer dove and swam out to sea, Natsilane saw the two young men riding safely toward him upon the backs of the sea lions. No longer was Whale Killer an enemy of people.

To this day, when October comes, some say they can see Natsilane as he hunts riding astride the backs of two Whale Killers. Then he sings the old hunting songs. Others say, "It is only the wind blowing through the leaves of the yellow cedar."

Crab & the Water Animals

Naga
(India)

Crab, Minnow, Frog and Shrimp were friends who worked hard and cooperated well with one another. Each day, these four women went out to work in the rice fields. They sang many songs so the hard work of tending the fields passed quickly. Near the end of each day, one of the four friends would leave the others and go back to prepare a meal for everyone. When dinner was ready, she returned to the field and called her three friends in to eat. In this way, they took turns cooking for one another.

One evening it was Crab's turn to cook. As they were finishing their meal, Minnow said, "Crab, your cooking is by far the best of anyone's."

"Yes, indeed," said Shrimp.

"Without a doubt," Frog agreed.

"Thank you," said Crab. "I am glad that you have noticed how hard I work to make good meals for us all."

Frog, Minnow and Shrimp leaned toward one another and whispered quietly for a moment or two.

"Your meals are delicious! Would you consider cooking for us every day? We would be glad to have you do so."

"But what about my work in the rice fields?" asked Crab.

"We will do your work for the hours that you are away cooking."

"Yes, I would love to," said Crab.

There came the time of year when food was hard to find. One day, as Crab prepared the vegetables, she found that there was nothing left to add for flavoring. She pulled off one of her own legs and threw it into the pot. That evening, when Frog, Shrimp and Minnow were eating, they all remarked on what a tasty meal Crab had prepared. Each of Crab's friends helped herself to seconds.

"Thank you for giving your own leg for our meal," they said. "It is a great sacrifice."

Crab felt so good when she heard this praise that, in the coming days, she added one of her legs to each meal she cooked. One day she made *korma*, a dish using spicy yogurt and nut sauce, and on another she fashioned *channa*, a dish of garbonzo beans. Every day, when her friends came in from the rice fields, they sang her praises.

55

They laughed until the sun went down. Their sides ached.

"You are the most wonderful cook in all these parts," they said. "We are grateful for the fulfilling meals you present us after we work so hard in the fields."

Encouraged by their kind words, Crab kept using one of her legs to flavor each new meal. After a few more days, there was nothing left of Crab but her body—all of her legs had been cooked and served for dinner.

That evening, as Shrimp, Minnow and Frog waited for Crab to come and call them in for dinner, no one came. They began to worry.

"Where is Crab?" asked Frog. "She has usually announced that dinner is ready by now."

"It is not like Crab to be late. We should go find out if something has happened to her," said Minnow.

The three of them went to the kitchen and looked everywhere.

"Crab," they called, "where are you? It is time for dinner. Come out if you are hiding." But Crab had disappeared.

"I think she has gone off alone so that she can grow her legs back," said Frog. "After all, what can she accomplish without legs?"

"I am hungry," said Minnow. "We had better eat without her."

"Mmm, this smells good," said Shrimp as she lifted the lid off the curry that was cooking on the stove.

When the three of them peered over the lip of the pot, they saw that, having no legs left to add, Crab had used her entire body to flavor the meal. There she sat in the middle of the steaming curry.

When Frog, Minnow and Shrimp saw what a sacrifice Crab had made so that they could have a delicious meal, they looked at each other and began to chuckle. Then they started to laugh. Harder and harder they laughed until tears streamed from their eyes. The three of them thought this was so funny that they fell down and rolled upon the kitchen floor. Frog was bent over completely in her spasms. Minnow was shaking her head up and down. Every time Shrimp tried to get up she walked helplessly backward until she fell down again. They laughed until the sun went down. Their sides ached. The three friends were exhausted.

At last, when the laughter stopped, Minnow tried to move her head. But her neck, which had been long and thin, was so swollen she had to turn her entire body to look around. Frog attempted to stand up, only to find that her back was permanently hunched over and her eyes bugged out. Shrimp tried to walk toward the pot of curry, but she could no longer walk forward. All she could do was back up in the direction she wanted to go, just as she had done during her fit of laughter.

From that day on, Shrimp, Frog and Minnow could no longer work in the rice fields. The three of them took to a life in the water, where they were better able to survive. They have lived there ever since.

Crab & the Water Animals

The Tortoise & the Egrets

(TIBET)

THERE ONCE WAS A BEAUTIFUL LAKE with sun-drenched, sandy shores. Egrets and herons waded in the shallows in search of something to eat. Ducks swam on the surface and dove the deep waters to catch a meal of fish. Up on the bank lived a small tortoise who loved to swim out and sun himself on the tufts of grass that held their heads above the open water of his quiet cove.

One day, two egrets waded past Tortoise's favorite sunny tussock of grass. "Hello," said the Egrets.

"Hello to you," replied Tortoise. "What are you searching for?"

"We are trying to find some fish to eat," said one Egret.

Tortoise swam over to the Egrets and the three of them began to play games in the water. Each day, as the Egrets waded past Tortoise's sunning place, they joined together in play. Soon, they became the best of friends and were never far apart.

One day an Egret said, "Tortoise, why are you sunning yourself so high up from the water today?"

"I am in my usual place," Tortoise replied. "It's just that the water is not as high as it used to be."

It had been a hot, sunny springtime that led to a summer with little rain. Each day, it seemed, the water level dropped a little. In time, Tortoise's clumps of grass stood in dried-up, cracked mud flats. Instead of playing, Tortoise and the Egrets spent most of their time worrying about what would happen if the rains did not soon return.

"Without water," said one of the Egrets, "the fish will start to die. We will have no food to eat. In time, there will be no water to drink. Without food and water we will not be able to survive."

Tortoise became so upset that he could not even speak. "Where could I go?" he asked himself. "And how would I get there?"

One day, the Egrets flew down to greet Tortoise. "Friend," they said. "The birds have decided to move from here. They are going to travel to a place called the Lake of the Clouds. It never dries up there, no matter how long between the rains. We will certainly die if we stay here."

Tortoise began to cry. "I know that you must fly off to save yourselves," he sobbed, "but there is no way that I can go with you. I would surely die of thirst before I completed the long walk to the Lake of the Clouds." With sad eyes he looked up at his friends and said, "I will understand if you go. When the drought breaks and you return to this place, please find my shell and give me a decent burial." Even as Tortoise spoke these words, he knew his friends would not be able to leave him behind.

Tears welled up in the Egrets' eyes. "We cannot leave you behind," they said. "We will remain here until it rains once again."

One day passed, then another, and still the rain did not come. Each day, a relentless sun traveled across a hot, hazy sky. Trees dropped their withered leaves, and fish gathered in schools in the few cool, deep pools that remained.

"We are going to die if we do not leave soon!" said the Egrets to Tortoise.

"I know," he replied, "and I can no longer expect you to remain here with me. But isn't there some way that I could fly with you to the Lake of the Clouds? Surely, if we all think hard enough, we can figure something out."

The Egrets slogged back and forth along the mud flats that once were covered with cool water. They talked to each other in low whispers but shook their heads each time they found fault in a plan they were hatching. Finally, Tortoise saw the Egrets nodding their heads in agreement as they walked toward him.

"Tortoise, we have a plan that just might work."

"Tell me what it is!" said Tortoise excitedly. But, without a word, the Egrets flew away to carry out their plan.

"Hey, wait, don't leave me here!" Tortoise cried out. "I thought you had a plan!"

In a short while, the Egrets flew back and landed in front of Tortoise. Each of the birds was holding the end of a stick in its mouth. They placed the stick on the dried up mud in front of Tortoise.

"What am I supposed to do with that?" asked Tortoise impatiently.

"We will keep this stick between us and hold it in our beaks. You bite onto the center and hold tight as we take off and fly to the Lake of the Clouds."

"What a clever plan," said Tortoise. "You are the best friends and the smartest birds I have ever met."

"But you cannot talk while we are flying together," warned the Egrets. "You must keep your mouth closed at all times."

"There is no way that I will open my mouth," Tortoise declared.

"There is very little food and water left," said one of the Egrets. "I think we should leave at once."

With that, they grabbed the stick firmly in their beaks. Tortoise walked over to the stick and bit down as hard as he could. It was a strange sight as the three friends rose up from the mud flats, circled in the sky and waved good-bye to the lake they had called home for so long.

Higher and higher they soared, borne on the great, wide, steady wings of the Egrets. They passed over many beautiful places as they flew. The forest at the edge of the lake turned into great stretches of waving grasslands dotted

The Tortoise & the Egrets

with tall trees. Dried-up riverbeds snaked over the land. They flew over a cliff that dropped steeply into a gorge through which trickled a once-mighty river.

At last, in the distance, they could see that tall, snow-capped mountains ringed the sky ahead.

"That is where we will find the Lake of the Clouds," said one of the Egrets from the corner of its beak as it motioned with a foot.

Down below, some people were working hard, trying to scratch out a living on their parched, dusty farmland. One of them looked up and saw something odd.

In the distance, they could see that tall, snow-capped mountains ringed the sky.

"Look, up in the sky! That is a very intelligent tortoise," she shouted. "Look how it has convinced the egrets to carry him as they fly. All he has to do is hold on by his mouth while they do all the work."

The Egrets ignored the remark. But when Tortoise heard this, he began to think that he was smart, indeed. "It is true," he thought to himself. "I am more clever than I thought!"

The three of them flew on to where the melting snows flowed down from the mountain slopes. Some children were playing in a stream. One child looked up when he saw the reflection of Tortoise and the Egrets in the surface of the stream water.

"There, above us!" he cried out. "Those must be the smartest egrets I have ever seen. They have discovered a way to make a tortoise fly!"

When he heard this, Tortoise became hurt, then angry. He began to think, "Those children do not know anything. How dare they imagine that the Egrets thought of this plan. I am certainly the most intelligent one of us all and I am not going to pass before I let those children know it."

At that moment, Tortoise yelled as loud as he could, "It was me … ."

But once his mouth opened, Tortoise realized his mistake. He began to fall, tumbling head over tail. Down, down, down he went, faster and faster. At last, and with a good deal of luck, he landed with a great splash in a deep pool upstream from where the children were playing.

When the Egrets looked down and saw that their friend was safe, they continued on their journey to the Lake of the Clouds. Since that day, tortoises have always kept their feet on the ground and none has ever again taken to the sky.

60

The Porpoise Wife

(Caroline Islands/Micronesia)

The two porpoises glided beneath the ocean's surface. Each time they needed a breath, they leaped out of the water in a graceful arc. From the highest point of each leap, they could see an island. A group of men were dancing there.

"If we come back to that island at night," said one porpoise to the other, "we may be able to see the dancing from close by."

"Let us return after the sun has set," said the other.

When the stars shone brightly in the sky, the two porpoises swam into the calm waters near the island. Once in the shallows, they took off their tails and walked up on the beach in the form of young women. Quietly, they sneaked up behind a grove of palm trees near where the men were dancing around a fire. For a long time, the porpoise girls sat mesmerized by the lapping flames and rhythms of the dancers' movements. Suddenly, the dance was over. The girls ran toward the beach so the men would not find them. They put on their tails and swam away from the island.

The sun rose over the atoll the next morning and shone down onto emerald waves breaking gently upon the sand. One of the island men strolled toward the shore near where the porpoise girls had walked by starlight. He was gathering palm sap for use in making a sweet drink called *hachi*, or palm toddy. As he reached down to gather the sap, the young man saw footprints in the sand. He looked closely, but the tracks left by the porpoise girls were strange to him. "I have never seen tracks like these," thought the young man.

That night, by the light of a crescent moon, the porpoise girls swam back to the island. They removed their tails, hid them well and watched in human form until the island men were done dancing. While the men were still gathered around the fire, the porpoise girls sneaked to the beach, pulled their tails on and slipped into their sea home.

The girls so enjoyed the dancing men that they returned the next night, and the night after that. When the young man who was gathering palm sap saw the unusual traces in the sand for the fourth morning in a row, his curiosity grew strong. "I must find out who or what is making these strange tracks," he thought. "They are not human, and I do not know of any animal that leaves such traces in the sand."

61

On the fifth night when the two porpoises again came ashore, removed their tails and appeared as two young women, the young man was hiding nearby. His eyes widened when he saw the girls emerging. Once the porpoise girls had walked away toward the sound of the dancing men, the young man found their two tails. He picked up one of the tails, carried it home and hid it in the loft of his house.

When the dancing was over the girls ran back down to the shore.

"I cannot find my tail," whispered one of the girls. "Did I not leave it here next to yours?" she asked her friend.

"Yes, it was right there," replied the other porpoise girl as she put her tail on.

"Please help me find my tail."

"But I think I hear someone coming," said her friend, who had once more taken on the form of a porpoise and was already slipping into the water.

Soon, the frightened porpoise girl was left alone on the beach. All night long she searched frantically for her tail, but could not find it.

When the sky began to glow with morning light, the young man walked down to the beach. He found the porpoise girl sitting up against the palm tree. Tracks of dried tears streaked her face. As soon as the man approached, the girl stood up and began to run away.

"Do not be afraid," he cried out. "I mean you no harm. You are so beautiful. I would like you to become my wife."

The porpoise girl stopped and turned toward the young man, "I don't know what to do. Somehow, my tail has disappeared. Without it I must remain on this island."

"I will help you," said the young man.

"Very well," she replied, "If I must live on this island, I will marry you."

From the first day, and throughout their life together, her husband had asked that she not visit the loft between the ceiling and the roof of the house. His wife honored this wish.

A short time after they became husband and wife, the porpoise girl found that she was expecting a child. She gave birth to a beautiful young girl whom she and her husband loved very much. Still, the porpoise girl rarely laughed or smiled. Often, her husband would catch her sitting for hours with their daughter, staring longingly out to sea. She was especially restless when the porpoises were frolicking offshore. One season faded into another and, in a few years, the melancholy young wife had a son.

One day, her husband and son went out fishing. The porpoise wife looked around and saw that the house was cluttered and needed to be cleaned. She picked up her husband's old fishing gear and climbed the ladder so that she might store it in the loft. Tucked away in the corner of the loft, she saw a

62

She sat for hours with their daughter, staring longingly out to sea.

strange package, something wrapped in palm leaves. As the brown, brittle palm fronds crinkled to pieces in her hands, the young woman's long lost tail was revealed. It was dried and wrinkled, and some small creatures had nibbled on its edges, but she could see it was her own.

Excitedly, the porpoise wife carried her daughter and her tail down to the beach. She bathed her daughter and gently rubbed turmeric on her skin. The child sensed that her mother was going away, and she began to cry.

"Mommy is going to leave now," she said as tears rolled down her cheeks. "I am really a porpoise, and I must return to live with my people in the sea. If your father and brother, or any of the men of the island ever catch a porpoise in their nets when they are fishing, you and your brother and father must be sure to see that it is released. You must never eat any porpoise if a fisherman brings one back."

She held the child to her breast. "Daddy will take good care of you. Whenever you want to see me, come down to the shore and blow on this seashell. Then watch the horizon. When you see me leaping up from the waves, I want you to know how much I love you, and that I would have stayed with you if I had been able."

The young woman took her tail and carefully rubbed it with salt water. Gradually, the skin took on its original color. It was sleek and shiny, just as it

The Porpoise Wife

had been several years ago on the night when she had last seen it. She gave her daughter one last kiss and said a final good-bye. Then the porpoise wife waded into the water and put on her tail. A porpoise once more, she swam out to sea.

As the young man and his son were fishing from their boat, a porpoise began to circle and call to them. It swam round and round the boat and made a lamenting cry. In time, a sadness came over her husband's face and his eyes glistened. He realized that this was his wife. She had found her tail at last.

"Do not worry," he told her, "I will take good care of our son and daughter. Please forgive me for deceiving you all these years; it was because of your beauty and the love I felt for you. It is time you returned to your people. We will miss you and keep you in our hearts."

The porpoise leaped high, gave one last cry, then returned to the sea. Quickly, the father and son made for shore, where they found and comforted the little girl. From that day forth, that father, daughter and son considered porpoises to be members of their own family. They never hunted or ate porpoises and always treated them with kindness and respect. Whenever a porpoise was caught in someone's net, they did everything they could to see that it was rescued and released unharmed to the sea. So it has been to this day among the generations descended from that family—the people of the Porpoise Clan of the Caroline Islands.

Hummingbird & the Selfish Fox

Yamana
(Tierra del Fuego)

A LONG, DRY SPELL CAME TO THE LAND. Water was scarce. Plants withered and animals were dying from thirst. *Čilawáia*, the Fox, found the one remaining lagoon of water. As quickly as he could work, Čilawáia built a strong fence around the lagoon so no one else could enter. When the fence was finished, Čilawáia hid inside and would only allow his relatives to enter and drink the water.

When the other animals heard about Čilawáia's lagoon, they traveled there in search of water. "Please let us enter to take a drink," they begged. "We are going to die if we do not have some water."

"Go away," said Čilawáia. "Why should I help you? Besides, there is not enough water for everyone."

More and more animals died from thirst. Again the survivors approached Čilawáia. The animals offered to trade some fresh meat for water, but Čilawáia turned them away. By now the animals were so weak with thirst that they were dragging themselves around outside the fence surrounding Čilawáia's lagoon.

As a final effort, the animals called on the tiny hummingbird, *Omóra*, to help them. Even though she was very small, Omóra was brave and fearless. She had been able to help the animals during a moment of great need long ago. In a short time, with a whir of wings, Omóra appeared to the animals.

"How can I help you?" she asked. "What is wrong?"

"Čilawáia has built a fence around the last water!" someone cried. "We are dying of thirst, but Čilawáia is hoarding all of the water for himself and his relatives."

Omóra's wings were a blur as she flew off to find selfish Čilawáia. In a short time she was hovering over Čilawáia as he soaked in the water of the lagoon.

"Is it true that you refuse to give water from this lagoon to the other animals, even though the thirst is killing them?" asked Omóra.

"That is their problem," replied Čilawáia. "I found this water first and it is mine to do with as I wish. If I offered water to everyone I would not have enough to live on."

*"Is it true that you refuse to give water from this lagoon
to the other animals?" asked Omóra.*

Omóra flew off in a rage. She gathered her sling and a few pointed stones, then headed back to where Čilawáia was basking in the lagoon. All the other animals gathered around Čilawáia's fence to watch.

"This is your last chance Čilawáia," yelled Omóra. "Do you not care that the animals will die if you keep all of the water for yourself? It is hard to believe that you can be so selfish."

"Well, if me and my relatives are going to survive, the rest of the animals are just going to have to die of thirst. That is all I have to say. Go away Omóra."

As these last words came out of his mouth, Omóra shot a pointed rock from her sling directly at Čilawáia. He tried to jump out of the way, but he was too late. The stone killed Čilawáia instantly.

Earth Tales from Around the World

At that moment, the animals rushed forward, trampled the fence and ran screaming into the lagoon. They drank all the water they could hold. A sigh of relief arose from the crowd. But some of the birds who arrived late found the lagoon empty.

Síta, the horned owl, and the other birds, used their beaks and feet to gather mud from the bottom of the lagoon. Using all of their strength, they flew up and dropped the mud near the tops of the slopes in the nearby mountains. Wherever this mud landed, a small spring trickled out and flowed downhill. These springs joined into streams, then formed rivers that snaked through the valleys. Unlike the warm, muddy water of the lagoon, the water from these springs was cool and clear.

Ever since that time, streams and rivers have flowed down from the mountains. For those who live along the slopes, and in the nearby valleys, there is plenty of water to drink.

Hummingbird & the Selfish Fox

Lessons

See the "Activities" section for ideas on how to explore these lessons.

In **Natsilane & the Killer Whales** we visit the strange land under the sea and the fascinating things that live there. This tale explains the origin of the killer whale, porpoise, blackfish and dolphin. We learn some customs Tlingit hunters observe for treating animals with respect, and that hunted animals are kind to respectful hunters. We see how jealousy causes violent, unexpected events, and how justice prevails.

Crab & the Water Animals is a strange, twisted tale. It explains how Frog, Shrimp and Minnow came to live underwater. Crab sacrifices and gives freely of herself as she takes satisfaction from pleasing the others. This Naga story from India shows that cooperation works when everyone does their part, and that others do not always appreciate the gifts they receive. If we don't show gratitude, no good will come of it.

In the Tibetan story, **The Tortoise & the Egrets**, a great drought shows how important water is for the animals' survival. It reveals that animals often migrate as they search for new sources of water. The way the Egrets agree to bring Tortoise to a distant source of water shows how hardship can inspire others to help one another. When Tortoise falls as he tries to tell the children that *he* thought of the plan to travel by hanging from a stick, he shows how false pride can be our downfall, literally.

The Porpoise Wife is a haunting tale of marriage between beings from two different worlds—the land and the sea. The Porpoise Wife becomes sad and lonely when forced to live on land. She misses friends, family and the sea. We can adapt, but it is hard to change our true nature. This story explains the origin of the Porpoise Clan in the Caroline Islands of Micronesia and why these people treat porpoises with respect. It reminds us that people are more closely related to animals than we tend to believe. The story also shows how curiosity can get us into trouble, but can also help solve our problems.

This Yamana story, **Hummingbird & the Selfish Fox**, shows that it is important to share water, and other life-giving resources, especially during a drought and at other times when there is little to go around. If we do not share willingly, violent things often occur to restore the balance. This tale explains where the clean, clear water of springs, streams and rivers came from, and how it is meant for all to share.

68

Five

Seasons & Weather

Earth & Sky Reconcile

Yoruba
(NIGERIA)

Earth and Sky once lived together in a vast land covered by a lush, green forest. All the plants and animals of the forest existed here in peace with the human beings. Monkeys called from where they foraged in the trees. Birds of many colors filled the air with song. Insects flew among the sweet flowers, and the lion slept in the shade along a riverbank.

Then, things began to change. The people and animals who hunted held a meeting. It was decided that they would burn the bush and capture the animals who fled the fire. When the time came, a line of fire was set upwind from the forest and the lapping flames spread quickly. The animals and the human beings who set the fire gathered downwind to capture what they could.

After the fire had passed, a search began. From the highest nest in the treetops to the deepest burrow in the forest floor, the people and the animals looked for many days, but no food could be found.

Finally, someone caught and killed one meager rat. It was the custom in this region to take the first game to the most powerful beings—Earth and Sky. The rat was wrapped carefully in a fresh leaf. A procession of animals and people carried the rat to where Earth and Sky lived.

"Since I am the oldest being, the rat should be given to me," Earth declared.

"No, it should not," responded Sky. "As everyone knows, I am older than Earth. The rat should be mine."

For many hours Earth and Sky argued over who should receive the rat. Finally, Sky became so angry that he flew from that place and vowed never to return. Higher and higher he flew to a new home far above Earth and all who lived upon her.

At first, no one noticed that Sky was gone. Everything seemed to go along as it always had. Sun rose in the east and made his journey across the sky each day. Moon continued to light the darkness with her cool light. The stars shone overhead.

Then people found that the rivers were running low. Crops began to wither and the leaves of wild plants drooped. Children no longer sang the happy tunes when the rains fell. Hungry women stopped bearing children. Dust swirled in the dry air and choked the birds as they tried to sing their songs.

Earth called a meeting of all the animals, birds, insects and people.

"What are we going to do?" asked Earth. "The rains have failed us. We cannot go on this way much longer. Soon this drought will turn to a killing thirst, and a famine will be upon us."

The crowd opened a path, and a person of vision stepped forward to speak. "I have looked into the heart of Nature," she said. "Is it not true that you have quarreled with Sky?" she asked of Earth.

"Yes, we fought over who should receive the rat that was captured in the forest," said Earth.

"That is the reason the rains have not returned," she replied. "There is only one way that the rains can be made to return."

"And what is that?" asked Earth.

"You must give the rat to Sky," she ordered.

The hardships that Earth was experiencing were so great that she agreed to give the rat to Sky.

"Who among you will carry out this honorable deed?" Earth asked of all who had gathered.

"I will try," offered Hawk. He picked up the rat and flew up toward Sky in great spirals. While they watched Hawk carry the rat to Sky, the people, birds, animals and insects sang this song:

> *Earth and Sky once argued,*
> *the truth must now be told.*
> *Sky said he was ancient*
> *and Earth said she was old.*
> *Sky fled to the skyland*
> *then he withheld the rain.*
> *Leaves and rivers withered*
> *when drought and famine came.*
> *Wheat and barley failed*
> *and yams dried in the dust.*
> *Now Hawk is flying high*
> *to reach the Sky, he must.*

As soon as the song was finished, Hawk's strength was used up and he returned to Earth carrying the rat.

"Can anyone bring this rat to Sky?" asked Earth.

"Give the rat to me," said Hornbill. "I will bring it to Sky."

Again, as Hornbill flew upward, the people and animals sang their song. But Hornbill also flew back down without reaching Sky. One after another the birds tried to bring the rat to Sky, but no one had the strength or endurance to fly high enough.

"Now it is my turn," said Vulture's raspy voice.

72

At that moment black clouds formed. Lightning and thunder seemed to split the heavens.

"How can you succeed where we have failed?" laughed all the other birds. They did not have much hope that Vulture could accomplish this challenging feat because she was not thought to be the smartest of birds.

Before their laughter faded, Vulture picked up the rat and flew toward Sky.

"I can no longer see her," said one of the monkeys. "I wonder if she has reached Sky?"

At that moment a clap of thunder rolled across the land and everyone knew that Vulture had knocked on Sky's door.

Earth & Sky Reconcile

"Who are you and what do you want here?" asked the guard who watched the door that led to Sky's home.

"I am Vulture and I have come to see Sky. I have a very important message from Earth."

"Come in," said the guard as he led Vulture to where Sky was seated. When Vulture was brought before Sky, she knelt down in respect and reverence.

"Why have you made the long, difficult journey from Earth?" demanded Sky.

"I have come to seek your forgiveness from Earth," Vulture explained. "Earth has now learned that you are indeed the eldest, and that the rat rightfully belongs to you." Vulture came forth and placed the rat at Sky's feet.

Sky laughed so hard that peals of thunder shook Earth below. "Very well," said Sky. "Earth is forgiven. The rains will fall once more. Rivers will run with sweet water. The crops and leaves of the forest will grow lush and green. Songs of joy will ring from the throats of the children, and women will again give birth. People will dance and celebrate as birdsongs fill the air. Come, Vulture, I have something to give you."

Sky led Vulture into the beautiful land above. "Here," said Sky. "Take these three gourds. Break the first one as you are leaving the door to my land. When you have flown halfway back to Earth, break open the second gourd. Once you have reached Earth, break open the third."

With many thanks, Vulture said good-bye to Sky. As she passed through the door to leave the land of Sky, Vulture split open the first gourd. At that moment black clouds formed. Lightning and thunder seemed to split the heavens.

"Now we are sure that Vulture has pleased Sky with his gift," said the people and animals who waited below.

Halfway down to Earth, Vulture broke open the second gourd, and a light rain began to fall. Down below, everyone rejoiced as gentle raindrops quenched the parched land.

When Vulture's feet finally touched Earth, she cracked open the third gourd. Torrents of rain fell from Sky, and everyone ran to seek shelter. Vulture, too, looked for shelter from the rain. She poked her head into the doorways of people's houses. She tried to enter the burrows and nests of the animals. But each time she stuck her head into someone's home, they pulled at the feathers on her head and told her to leave. In a short time, Vulture's head was completely bald.

74   When, at last, Vulture could find no one to shelter her from the rain, she flew to the highest branch of a tall tree. "So this is how you repay me for the sacrifice that I have made," she said in anger. "From this day forth you will have to work hard to repay every act of kindness and generosity you receive."

A thousand generations have passed since that long-ago quarrel between Earth and Sky. Yet, it is still hard to get anyone to help when you need a favor unless you offer something of value in return.

Nanabozho Brings the Seasons

Anishinabe /Ojibwa or Chippewa
(CANADA AND UNITED STATES)

BACK IN THE EARLY DAYS, Nanabozho and his brother, Peepaukawis, were walking around.

"Let us have a race," said Nanabozho, who always beat his brother in a contest.

"Very well," said Peepaukawis.

The two brothers began running toward the north. Nanabozho, who ran as swift as a gale in a storm, soon passed his brother and left him far behind.

Wherever Nanabozho ran, the good weather came upon the land; Earth and Sky came to peace with one another. As Peepaukawis followed his brother, he noticed that a patch of colorful flowers sprouted in every place Nanabozho's moccasins touched the soil. Because Nanabozho brought the warm winds and the sunshine, the plants and animals were glad to see him.

"Our friend Nanabozho is coming," they said. "Hello, oh Manitou!" called the squirrel and the beaver, the rabbit, fox and bear. Up in the treetops, the birds and the leaves greeted Nanabozho. "Welcome to this place," they said as he passed below. "Thank you for the kind weather."

Peepaukawis fell farther and farther behind in the race. When he heard the living things praising Nanabozho, he envied his brother. Peepaukawis became red with jealousy. "I will show them," he said. He stopped on the banks of the great river, took handfuls of water and threw them into the air.

"Come North Wind. Come West Wind and bring the foul weather. Cause fingers to reach from the sky. Cover the land with sleet and snow. Blow clouds across the face of Sun so Nanabozho might become lost. Come South Wind, blow long and hot and dry across the open places until the corn and wild rice are bent and brown."

Up ahead, Nanabozho shivered as clouds covered Sun. Then he turned around, gazed up at the sky and laughed. Hearing this, the clouds pulled back and Sun shown warm and bright.

At last, Nanabozho came to the Great Lakes. There, along the shore, he rested for the night. As Nanabozho slept, Peepaukawis ran past in the darkness. Again the cold, blustery winds began to blow. The clouds blotted out the moon and stars.

75

*A patch of colorful flowers sprouted
where Nanabozho's moccasins had touched the soil.*

When Nanabozho was awakened by the howling, icy winds, he knew that Peepaukawis had gone by. At once, Nanabozho leaped to his feet and ran toward the North. He passed Peepaukawis and, for a few days, the weather once more turned warm and pleasant. To this day that short period of good weather is called Indian Summer. But, because Nanabozho and his brother were running to the north, winter came at last. The weather turned cold and the land froze hard as flint.

The race between Nanabozho and Peepaukawis continues to this day. Good weather comes when Nanabozho is out in front. When Peepaukawis passes his brother, he brings the bad weather. That is why the weather is fickle in the north country, the home of the Anishinabe.

Nanabozho is the trickster-hero among the Anishinabe *(Ah-nish-ih-nah´-bey), whose name means "First Men." This people, who live in a vast part of north-central North America, are also known as the Ojibwa or Chippewa.*

76

Rainbow

Guajiro
(COLOMBIA AND VENEZUELA)

JUYA, MASTER OF THE RAIN, began the storm as a drizzle. Slowly, the drops grew in size and the rain became louder. Streams and rivers swelled their banks and flooded the land. Villages washed away in the strong currents. Many people and animals were drowning.

"It is time to stop the rain!" said Kasipoluin, Rainbow. Without her, the rain would never stop. Whenever Juya is about making the rain, Kasipoluin also comes out and watches him. She is the only one who can control Juya.

Now, the rain slowed until it was just a fine mist. Sun began to show overhead and Kasipoluin's bridge of colors arched across the sky.

"Look!" said a child, "Kasipoluin has come to visit. Let's go find out where her feet are touching the ground."

All the other children followed that child toward the end of the rainbow. On and on they ran. Kasipoluin was standing very far away. At times, she seemed to be running away from them just as fast as they were moving toward her. The children ran to the top of a small hill and looked down.

"There, look at that," cried one of the children. "I can see where Kasipoluin is standing."

In that very spot, the children saw the head of an enormous Maliwa crocodile laying on the ground. Like a great ribbon of colored smoke, Kasipoluin came from the mouth of the crocodile. The children could see the colors of *ishosü, malaukatsü* and *wüitüsü*—red, yellow and blue or green—and all those in between. The children were afraid, but they kept watching.

Juya, who is the enemy of crocodiles, saw Kasipoluin coming from the crocodile's mouth. He threw down a fiery bolt of lightning that struck the crocodile. When the smoke cleared, crocodile was gone and Kasipoluin's colors had faded from the sky. The children ran back to the village to tell their elders what they had seen.

There are many stories about where Kasipoluin, Rainbow, comes from. Some people say that she comes from the mouth of a snake, any snake, while others believe that she can only come from the sarulu boa. Juya's lightning kills many of the big snakes, which is why there are so few. In some beliefs, Kasipoluin projects from the mouth of an iguana. The tale of the rainbow serpent is also widespread among the Aboriginals of Australia.

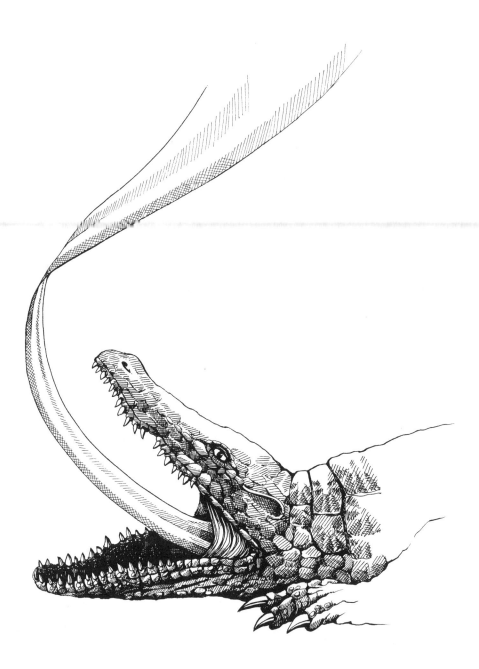

Like a great ribbon of colored smoke,
Kasipoluin came from the mouth of the crocodile.

The Wrath of March

(Italy)

A SAD-FACED YOUNG MAN walked through the countryside, his robes flowed and snapped in the chill wind. Past the vineyards and orchards, along the roads lined with quaint villas he strode.

"What is left for me to do?" thought the young man. "My time is almost over. Tomorrow, someone else will blow through the hills, rain on the young green leaves and bask in the glow of the sun. Still, there is none like me. When I am gone, the season will change. A new beginning is at hand."

A woman approached the young man in the lane. The hood of her cloak, which rustled in the wind, was drawn tightly around her face. She leaned into the cold breeze and shivered.

"Brrr!" she whispered as she drew near the young man.

"Do you not like this weather?" he asked. "It is the way of March, is it not?"

"Who can tell?" she complained in a hoarse voice. "March is a fickle month. One day a warm, soft breeze blows through sunlit vineyards. The next day it is as if winter has returned with a vengeance. I have caught a terrible cold, and it is all because of this miserable month of March."

The young man was not pleased. When the woman arrived in her dooryard, she gasped and began to curse. "Wretched March," she screamed shaking her fist at the sky. "Look what you have done." A brisk wind had toppled many of the trellises in her vineyard and her flower beds were littered with sticks and leaves.

Next, the young man met an elder farmer along the way. "Good sir," he said in greeting, "how has the month of March been treating the farmers?"

"You are a bit young to understand," said the old man. "I have seen every face of March during my many years. These harsh winds are also the first sign that spring is coming. Soon, the green shoots of barley will sprout and the fig trees will bloom. Even as we speak, the wildflower buds are beginning to swell and they will paint the fields with color. Why should we mourn that which is so full of promise?"

"Well said," responded the young man as he continued down the lane. When the farmer arrived home he walked between the fruit trees in his yard. There he saw the first honeybee buzzing around an early bloom. "Ahh," he thought, "good work my little friend. Thank you."

Young man March blew the coldest winds he could muster.

A smile spread across the young man's face as he walked briskly along. He came up behind a shepherd who was moving his flock of sheep to spring pasture.

"Good day," said the young man.

"And what is good about it?" asked the shepherd in anger. "What a menace is this month of March. Who can tell what it is going to do next? One day it is snow, the next warm sunshine. We have seen hail, sleet and rain in the past week alone! Even the winter months were kind to me and my sheep, but not March! Not one of my flock died until this wretched cold, wet weather arrived. A lamb became ill, and I could not find it in the thick fog until it was too weak to recover. It will be good riddance when this terrible month has passed. Be gone!" said the shepherd shaking his fist at the sky.

Hearing this, young man March became angry. He flew toward the setting sun in the west where his sister April lived. There he cried out:

> *April, my sweet sister,*
> *please help your brother dear.*
> *I want to teach a lesson*
> *to this unkind shepherd here.*
> *May I have three days*
> *of the month that you will bring?*
> *Then we shall hear the tune*
> *this ungrateful shepherd sings!*

Then came April's reply:

> *March, you are my brother,*
> *and your need I plainly see.*
> *Teach yon shepherd patience*
> *with these days of April, three.*

With three more days in hand, young man March blew the coldest winds he could muster. Thick, gray clouds covered the sky. Rain drenched the shepherd and his flock, then sleet and snow covered the pasture so that food was hard to find. More of his lambs, which were already weak with hunger, became sick and died.

"Very well!" cried the shepherd. "The wrath of March is great. You are the old and the new, the time of change between the cold winter and the warmth of summer. My humble apologies. I can see the wisdom of your ways!"

The next morning dawned sunny and warm. Birdsongs filled the air, and insects hummed a chorus of welcome to sister April.

The Wrath of March

A Basket of Friendship

(KOREA)

THE RAIN WAS FALLING SO HARD as Hajin walked that he pulled his hat down tight to shelter his eyes and rolled up his pant legs to keep them out of the mud. It was the Seventh Day of the Seventh Month, and Hajin was traveling down the road to visit his friend Chipo. He saw the young woman walking toward him with a basket in her hand. In the basket was a small pair of shoes.

"Hajin, is that you?" asked the familiar voice of his friend.

"Yes, of course," he replied. "What are you doing out in this rain? Your clothes are soaking wet. Why did you take your shoes off?" he asked somewhat sternly.

When he looked closer, Hajin could see that Chipo was crying. "Have you fallen? Where did that mud on your dress and on your feet come from? Are you hurt?"

"I just tried to cross the stream on my way to Hunchback Mountain," she replied, "but the water is so high that I could not get through. I don't know what I am going to do."

"What do you mean?" asked Hajin.

"If I do not reach the old house where the mulberry tree grows, all of my silkworms are going to die. They need the mulberry leaves to eat."

"Please, give me the basket," said Hajin. "In a little while I will be back with a basket full of mulberry leaves." He extended his hand and a small stream of water ran down his arm. Chipo handed him the basket and he ran off through the driving rain in the direction of Hunchback Mountain.

Once Hajin reached the river, he began to walk upstream. Leaves, sticks and whole trees were floating in water that was red with clay. Several magpies flew up from the branches of a tree on the opposite shore. Hajin could see them calling, but their voices were drowned out by the sound of the rushing water. Hajin kept slipping as he made his way carefully along the steep bank.

At last, Hajin came to where the river normally was just a stream that flowed through a narrow valley between the two mountains. Water that was usually ankle deep was now up to his chest. Great torrents flowed down from every side of the steep slope as if the hillside was a giant waterfall. Still, Hajin leaped into the swirling waters and waded across. When he was almost across, he slipped on the round rocks but was just able to grab a large root hanging from the opposite bank. Hajin pulled himself ashore and collapsed in a dripping heap.

After a brief rest, Hajin continued on the narrow, rocky trail until he reached the old house. He remembered the old stories about ghosts living in the roof of that house, and he shivered. In the backyard, Hajin found the ancient mulberry tree with its great branches arching overhead. Into the basket he laid each leaf with care, layer after layer, pressing them down as they built up. At last, the basket was full, and he replaced the lid.

Before he started back, Hajin stood under the mulberry arbor. In the distance, he could see that the stream had risen even higher, and its waters were raging. "It will be impossible for me to cross here now," he thought. "I would be carried away and drowned. I shall have to walk up the steepest slopes of Hunchback Mountain and cross even farther upstream."

With great care, Hajin crept along the slanted, mossy banks, holding onto each tree, root and rock to steady his balance. One slip and he would go tumbling down into the angry torrent. He came to a place where the stream valley was very narrow.

"If I hold onto the top of that elder tree," he thought, "I will be able to swing over onto the other side of the stream." Hajin scrambled up the elder tree and leaned out over the stream. With a great cracking sound, the elder tree, which was rotten inside, gave way and sent Hajin falling hard onto the opposite bank. He landed on a muddy slope, slid down and was caught as he struck his hip on a large rock. Bruised, muddy and with torn trousers, Hajin smiled as he looked down and saw that he still held the basket of mulberry leaves safely in his hand. Slowly, limping a little, Hajin picked his way down the trail toward the cart road that led home and to where Chipo was waiting.

It was not long before the raindrops grew smaller, and the wind quieted. When Hajin came to the bridge, he paused and looked over the railing at the swollen river. At that moment, he felt pride well up within his breast as he considered what he had accomplished. Whistling and swinging the basket in triumph, Hajin trotted homeward.

When Chipo saw Hajin coming, she ran out to meet him, using a lotus leaf for an umbrella. "You have done it!" she screamed jumping up and down. "My silkworms are going to live because you have brought back the mulberry leaves."

With a sense of ceremony, Hajin held out the basket of mulberry leaves and offered it to Chipo. He and Chipo both laughed as she took the basket into her hands. "Thank you, Hajin."

As they began to walk back to Chipo's house, she said, "Here, let me share this lotus leaf with you so that your head is covered."

"No, thank you," he said laughing. "By now I am wetter than the rain itself. Use the umbrella to keep yourself dry."

83

Hajin held out the basket of mulberry leaves and offered it to Chipo.

At that moment, Hajin no longer felt cold, wet or tired. His eyes caught a glance from Chipo as she smiled at him. Hajin realized that if it were not for the wind, the rain and the hardship of his journey, he would not feel this deep contentment. "How could it be," he thought, "that these things, of which everyone complains, could make me so happy?"

Earth Tales from Around the World

"You look like the poor Shim Chung in the story when she was eaten by the water dragon!" said Chipo.

At that moment, lacy spots of sunlight dappled the leaves of the pomegranate tree beneath which they were walking.

"The sky is clearing!" said Hajin as he narrowed his eyes to look closer.

"I have never seen anything so beautiful. My mother says that when the sun shines through the rain, the tiger will soon get married."

When they arrived at the bamboo gate in front of Chipo's house, the girl turned to Hajin and said, "I must go feed these leaves to my silkworms." She looked admiringly at the soaking, muddy friend who stood before her in his torn, green-stained trousers. Then she turned up the walk, cradling a basket full of friendship.

85

Lessons

See the "Activities" section for ideas on how to explore these lessons.

In **Earth & Sky Reconcile**, the Yoruba explore the origin of thunder, lightning and rain. This story shows that rain is needed for the Circle of Life to continue in the dry lands of Nigeria. It is believed that one must offer gifts to Sky so that rain will continue to fall, and that Nature must be treated with respect and reverence. When the people and animals pull the feathers from Vulture's head, she learns that her selfless deed is not appreciated. To this day, because of those people's and animals' ingratitude, good deeds must be repaid.

Nanabozho Brings the Seasons, a story from the Anishinabe, explores the changing seasons. Nanabozho brings warm weather and sunshine. His brother, Peepaukawis, causes cold, sharp winds to blow and freeze the land as they carry sleet, snow and ice. Peepaukawis also brings heat and drought. This story tells how nature responds to the seasons—the balance of weather that is both harsh and kind.

The Guajiro story **Rainbow** tells of the continuing struggle between Juya, Master of the Rain, and Kasipoluin, Rainbow, the only one who can stop the heavy rains and floods. The story explains where Kasipoluin comes from, and that she brings good weather. In the end, Juya strikes Kasipoluin with a bolt of lightning and she disappears.

The Wrath of March shows what happens in the natural world during the time in between the seasons of winter and spring. This Italian tale tells how our view of the world around us is the reason we experience the world the way we do. March rewards those who appreciate the changing weather and punishes those who only praise the weather when it is to their liking.

In this Korean story, **A Basket of Friendship**, a young boy named Hajin turns a hike through heavy rain, across a raging river and over treacherous, slippery mountain trails into a great adventure. He embraces these hardships and perseveres in order to accomplish something for his dear friend, Chipo, who is in need. He achieves a sense of accomplishment, satisfaction and pride and learns to appreciate harsh weather. As in many other stories in this book, the number seven is important.

Six

Plants

The Bay-Tree Girl

(GREECE)

A LONELY WOMAN WAS WALKING ALONG the shore of a lake. She stopped and looked at the green fingers of tree branches that reached out toward the water. The branches of the bay tree bore tiny, black berries.

"I pray thee, God, please give me a child," said the woman. "Make her as beautiful as the fruit of the bay tree, and with love as overflowing as the waves that wash upon this shore." In time, God granted the woman's wish.

The woman loved her daughter completely. Because the child was so small, her mother had to be careful not to lose her. One sunny morning, the woman could not find her daughter. She looked everywhere, retracing each step she had made the day before. Finally, she went down to the bank of a nearby brook to wash clothes. As the woman unfolded the garments, her tiny daughter fell out unnoticed and landed near the clear, cool waters.

Many years later, a prince and his entourage, who were returning from battle in a distant land, camped along the shores of that stream.

"This is a good place to rest," said the tired prince. "Let us eat our meal beneath the graceful branches of this tufted bay tree." In a short time the servants had set a table and placed a meal upon it. After the prince had finished eating, he lay back against the trunk of the bay tree and slept.

The next morning, as the prince awoke and stretched, he noticed that the remains of his meal had been eaten.

"Who would eat my food while I slept?" he demanded of his servants.

"It was not us," they insisted. "Why don't we stay another night and see if the thief returns?"

That evening, the prince ate part of his meal and left a portion upon each plate. He then rested against the bay tree in mock slumber while the brook sang its gentle tune and the leaves rustled in the evening breeze. As the moon reached high in the starry sky, an enchanting young girl stepped from the branches of the bay tree. The moon paled next to her beauty. From plate to plate she crept, sampling a bit of food from each. When she was satisfied, the girl began to retrace her steps toward the tree.

Swiftly, the prince arose, took the girl by the shoulders, faced her and asked, "Who are you and why are you eating my food?"

"Please, let me go," she cried. "I did not mean you any harm."

The prince released her at once. He could not stop looking at her radiant beauty. "Please forgive me," he said. Their eyes met in a long silence. Both felt as if they had known each other all their lives. "Stay with me tonight," asked the prince. "Sit by the stream and watch the moon dancing in the ripples."

"Very well, but I must return to my tree before sunrise." At that, the prince drew the girl close, and they kissed.

An enchanting young girl stepped from the branches of the bay tree.

Just before sunrise, the prince said, "Now, I must go back to my own country. In a short time, I will return. Then, I would like to take you back to become my wife."

"Yes, I will be your wife. But you must promise to kiss no one while you are gone. Should you kiss another, you will forget that we ever met. Good-bye, my love, until we meet again."

The prince, eager to return at once, summoned his soldiers and began the journey home. When he met his mother and father, the king and queen, they rushed forward to kiss him. The prince was careful to avoid their kisses, and those of everyone he met. That evening, he lay down exhausted and slept deeply. His godfather, who had just learned of the prince's return, walked quietly into the room where he slept. He bent down and kissed his beloved godson.

When the prince awoke at sunrise, his memory of the Bay-Tree Girl was gone. Even so, he knew that something was missing in his life. The young man lost his appetite and slept restlessly. After several weeks, he became sickly and depressed.

"We must do something to help him," said his mother. "I am beginning to fear for his life." The king and queen called the best doctors from the nearby villages, but none could heal the prince.

As the prince was wasting away, the Bay-Tree Girl went searching for him. On the day he left her, she had returned to the tree and asked, "Little Bay Tree, please part your branches so that I may come in."

"I am sorry, little one," answered the Bay Tree. "You have been kissed by a prince and passed the night together along the banks of the stream. You can no longer enter here."

90

"Please," cried the girl, "I have no other home." Then, the Bay-Tree Girl began to cry. No matter how long she wept and pleaded with the Bay Tree, it would not allow her to enter.

Forgotten by the prince and rejected by her own tree, the Bay-Tree Girl wandered about the countryside for many weeks. At last, she came to the kingdom that was home to the prince. She met a stranger who told her that the prince was so weak he was near death. The Bay-Tree Girl trimmed her hair short and dressed in the hooded robes of a healer. With a flask filled with a colorful liquid tucked under her arm, she made her way toward the palace.

The Bay-Tree Girl knocked on the palace gate and a servant answered.

"Whom do I address?" asked the servant.

"I am a physician," she said. "I heal the wounds of the heart."

The servant went to tell the queen who was calling.

"None of the physicians have been able to cure my son," she said in despair. "Why should this one be any different?"

But the prince overheard the conversation between the queen and the servant outside his door. "Please, bring the physician at once," he demanded.

When the hooded figure entered his room, the prince asked, "From whence have you come?"

"A long journey hence," answered the girl. "There is a river along whose banks grows a bay tree."

"What news do you bring me, healer?" he asked.

"On the banks of that river a girl knelt crying, as many tears as there are leaves on the branches of the bay tree. I heard her say, 'Dear God, I have no home and my love has forsaken me. What must I do?'"

At the sound of these words, the prince fainted. The Bay-Tree Girl, still in her disguise, opened the bottle and sprinkled some of the liquid upon the prince's face. When he revived, he asked again, "What news do you bring me, healer?"

"On the banks of a river a girl knelt crying, as many tears as there are leaves on the branches of the bay tree. I heard her say, 'Dear God, I have no home, and my love has forsaken me. What must I do?'"

When she had finished speaking, the girl unwrapped her garments. The prince saw that, underneath her robe, she wore the dress of the Bay-Tree Girl. The prince smiled for the first time in months, rose from his bed and embraced his love.

Over the coming days, the palace was decorated and meals prepared. Hundreds of guests appeared for the wedding of the prince and the lovely Bay-Tree Girl. After the pair was wedded, the feast and celebration carried on for forty days and nights. The couple shared a long and happy life together.

Kospi & the First Flowers

Tehuelche
(ARGENTINA)

IN A TIME WHEN THERE WERE NO FLOWERS in the world, there lived a beautiful girl named Kospi. Each morning, Kospi walked down to the lake and looked at its smooth, silvery surface. Kospi used the reflective water for a mirror by which to comb her long, straight black hair. When Kospi returned to the village, she joined the other women, both young and old, in daily work. Often, the women wove fiber mats, sewed or dyed blankets. On some days they gathered pigments to create paints of many hues.

Kospi was so alluring that young hunters came for great distances from the surrounding villages just to see her. It was said that, no matter how a young man felt when he arrived in Kospi's village, one glance at her smile would make him happy.

One foggy morning, Kospi took her comb and set off down the trail to the lake. As she bent over to gaze into the water, there was a brilliant flash of light. For some time, the light blinded Kospi. As she waited for her sight to return, she began to shiver. It seemed as if the cold South Wind had arrived at the wrong time of year. When she could see again, Kospi found that she had been transported to a vast cave in the hollow of an enormous glacier. A pale, bluish white light surrounded her. Kospi had been kidnapped by Lightning, the powerful being who ruled the mountains.

"Help!" Kospi screamed. "Can anyone hear me? I have been brought to this terrible place against my will. *Help!*" Over and over Kospi called out as she searched for a way to escape from the cave, but no one could hear her. Her grief was so great that she lost hope. Kospi laid down on the glacial ice and melted into it, becoming part of the frozen water itself.

When Lightning no longer heard Kospi calling, he went looking for her. But, because she had wandered off and had become part of the ice, he could not find her. Lightning thundered and his deep boom echoed into the valleys. Even though his cries were in vain, Lightning's voice stirred the rain into a frenzy. Torrents rushed down the valleys and melted the floes of ice. Kospi became part of the raging waters that flowed down the slopes toward the village. When, in time, the swollen streams and rivers ebbed within their banks, Kospi soaked into the earth on which her people walked each day.

Kospi used the reflective water for a mirror
by which to comb her long, straight black hair.

The following spring, a soft, warm North Wind began to blow. Slowly, the melted water of Kospi rose into the roots and stems of the plants all around her village. Every plant that grew from her water formed a lovely flower on the top of its stem. Each flower was the face of Kospi. From those flowers, and from every bloom that has since graced the hillsides, Kospi has looked out upon her people. To this day, when the Tehuelche see flower petals blooming, they say, "Look at the face of the beautiful Kospi. She has come to visit us once again."

Kospi & the First Flowers

Befriended by Flowers

(VIETNAM)

Each day as he walked home from school, the young poet Hà Nhân Giã passed the ruins of an old garden. "This must have been a beautiful garden," Hà thought as he peered over the tumbled heap of rocks, the remains of a magnificent wall.

One day, Hà heard voices coming from within the garden. The gentle laughing reminded him of soft rain falling. Through the tangle of leaves and colorful blossoms, Hà saw two beautiful young women. They scattered flower petals in his direction and threw ripe, sweet-scented fruits to him.

"Thank you," said Hà. "Where did you ever find these rare flowers?"

"We grow them here in our garden," replied the young women as they held up bunches of blooms and peered at Hà through the petals.

"Who are you and where is your family?"

"We once had a master, but he died years ago. Now we live here alone," said one of the young women. "My name is Dào Nũồng, and this is Liêũ Nũồng."

"Would you like to visit me after school?" asked Hà.

"Yes, very much," they replied.

That afternoon, Hà walked the young women home and made them some tea. As they sat and talked, Liêũ Nũồng spoke to him in verse.

> *Many faces pass*
> *beside our crumbling wall.*
> *But you're the only one*
> *who ever heard our call.*
>
> *Where others see the world*
> *of petal, leaf and vine,*
> *you have looked beyond*
> *to another place and time.*

When he heard these words, Hà understood that, like himself, his new friends were poets. Over the coming days and weeks, the three spent many evenings drinking tea and writing poems of friendship.

A warm breeze lifted the petals.

Time passed. Hà neglected his schooling and his other pursuits. When the warm, dry season arrived, Liêũ Nũõng and Dào Nũõng held a celebration in honor of their friend. Hà was led through the garden gate and along the fence until the three friends came to a gathering of people by the lily pond. Hà noticed that their brightly colored garments were made of a material finer than silk, as soft and cool to the touch as flower petals. As if in a dream, Hà floated about the garden of rare flowers. He met all the guests and learned their names. Shadows cast by the quivering light of the pine-pitch torches danced to a soft music played by unseen hands. On 'into the night Hà feasted on figs and sweet pastries as he sipped flower-scented wine. Never had he been so content. At sunrise, Hà awoke to find he was alone in the ancient garden.

That day, Hà's mother and father said they had arranged for him to marry a wonderful young woman. "I agree to marry her," said Hà, "but I would ask that the wedding be held some time in the future."

Hà visited Dào Nũõng and Liêũ Nũõng to tell them the news. "We are happy for you," they said, "but we will miss you."

"And I shall miss you," said Hà. "That is why I have asked to have the marriage delayed for a time." The two young women smiled.

One evening, when Hà had come to visit his two friends, they looked pale and weak. "We are ill with fever," they told him. "When the cool winds again bring the rain, we will die."

"Let me shelter you at my house," offered Hà.

"No, this is our fate," said the two young women.

Hà was so upset that he could not go home. He wandered aimlessly. A storm began to blow just as Hà reached the door of an elderly neighbor, whom he stopped to visit. As the wind howled outside the thin walls of the old man's house, Hà sat and told him the story of his life these past weeks. The elder's expression was grave.

When Hà fell silent, his neighbor spoke. "A scholar once lived in that house and tended the beautiful garden of rare flowers that you speak of. More than twenty years have passed since his death. During that time, the abandoned house and garden have fallen into ruin. Surely, you have seen the restless spirits of the rare flowers."

By now, the sun was painting the morning sky. Hà and the elder walked slowly toward the garden. Inside the gate they found nothing but an overgrown tangle of flowers crowded by weeds. As the old man named the rare flowers, Hà realized that these were the names of the people he had met at the celebration Dào Nũõng and Liêũ Nũõng had given in his honor.

"My flower friends have been kind," said Hà, "but I must resume my studies. I cannot live in their world, no matter how much it pleases me. Now I will return the friendship they have shared."

96

Hà sold his favorite musical instrument so he could hold an incense offering and prayer service in the garden. "This is the only way they will find peace," he said.

After the ceremony, Hà returned home. He lay down and fell into a deep sleep. In the place of dreams, Liêū Nūõng and Dào Nūõng came to visit. "Dear friend," they said, "our time together was filled with joy. You have been kind and generous with the prayers you offered us in the garden. Yet, our fate is that of a flower petal on the wind. Good-bye. We will not forget you."

Hà awoke and saw two pairs of delicate slippers at the foot of his bed, a token of remembrance from his friends. When Hà picked up the slippers, he found only flower petals. A warm breeze lifted the petals. Becoming tiny butterflies, they fluttered briefly about the young man's head, and were gone.

Befriended by Flowers

The Coming of Seeds & Gardens

Chorote
(ARGENTINA, BOLIVIA AND PARAGUAY)

LONG AGO, THERE WAS LITTLE FOOD in the world. The animals and people were starving. *Ijlió*, the Armadillo, decided to visit *Wuéla*, the Moon, and ask for his guidance.

Wuéla's children saw Ijlió approaching. "Who is that strange creature?" they asked their father.

"That is Ijlió," said Wuéla. "Ijlió, welcome to our home. You look weary from your journey."

"Hello, Wuéla," said Ijlió. "You are right, but I am more than tired. Food is scarce. The people and animals are starving. What are we going to do?"

"Daughter," Wuéla called, "Ijlió needs something to eat. Would you please offer him some melon?"

Wuéla's daughter handed a piece of melon to Ijlió. "You may eat this," she said. As soon as he took a few bites, Ijlió was completely full and satisfied.

"This is a wonderful food," he said. "It is delicious and filling."

"Now," said Wuéla, "take the rind and place it back into the melon where it came from." As soon as Ijlió replaced the piece of rind, the melon was once more complete, as if no one had taken a bite from it.

Wuéla offered Ijlió a taste of other garden crops, including maize, beans, melons and anco squash. Wuéla gave the seeds of all the crops to Ijlió.

"Take these seeds with you and plant them," said Wuéla. "You may eat the fruits and vegetables produced by these seeds. Even though the plants will die away, you must save some seeds from every crop. Plant the seeds each year when the rains and warm weather return. Just as the melon you ate became whole again, these seeds will produce another harvest. As long as you save and plant the seeds, you will have food to eat. Guard these seeds and you will be rewarded. Many different plants will grow. It is up to you to show others how to care for seeds and sow a garden."

Wuéla then took Ijlió for a walk. He gave him a taste of the fruit from many wild plants, including the cactus, *kixét*. "Whenever you eat fruit from these plants," Wuéla explained, "you must be sure to leave some behind for the future. These wild fruits are a gift that I will give you each year. You will not have to plant them."

98

"Thank you," said Ijlió. "I will remember everything you have shown me."

Ijlió returned home and waited for the growing season to arrive. Each day, the sun climbed higher in the sky, warming the moist earth. Finally, Ijlió saw that the season to sow seeds had arrived.

"It is time to plant the garden," Ijlió told his wife one morning. Then he picked up his bag of seeds and walked down to the clearing. In his bag, Ijlió carried seeds of maize, beans, squash and melons. As soon as Ijlió planted the seeds, they sprouted and began to grow. In a short time they produced a rich harvest of fruit and vegetables. *Wóiki,* the Fox, who was Ijlió's friend, hid and watched wide-eyed from the edge of the field.

Ijlió shared his harvest with Wóiki and all of the animals who lived nearby. But Wóiki was not satisfied. He waited all year for the next growing season to arrive.

"Now is my chance to grow my own garden and produce many kinds of fruits and vegetables," said Wóiki. "Once I have a big harvest I, too, will be able to find a wife like my friend Ijlió. I will plant exactly as Ijlió plants, because he had much food during last year's *nahkáp,* when the wild and cultivated crops ripened for the harvest."

From a distance, Wóiki followed Ijlió to his garden plot. When Ijlió began to prepare the soil for his seeds, Wóiki came in for a closer look.

"What are you doing here?" asked Ijlió.

"You are wise in the ways of the garden," said Wóiki. "I want to learn from you. Besides, you are good company, and I always look forward to seeing you."

At this, Ijlió became suspicious. "Nevertheless," Ijlió asked himself, "what harm can it do to show Wóiki how to grow crops? Perhaps it will keep him out of trouble."

"Very well," Ijlió said to Wóiki, "I will show you how it is done. I will sow my garden, and you may plant your garden next to mine."

Wóiki watched Ijlió plant the seeds of beans, melons, maize and anco squash. Ijlió carefully covered each seed with soil. Even though he was expecting it, Wóiki was amazed to see that the seeds began to grow immediately. By the time Ijlió reached the end of a row, the plants behind him had already sprouted. They continued to grow as he worked down the length of the garden.

From the corner of his eye, Ijlió watched Wóiki warily. With seeds in hand, Wóiki began to make planting holes with a stick. Instead of planting seeds in each hole, however, Wóiki ate them as he walked along.

99

Ijlió stopped planting and walked over to look at the rows that Wóiki had created. "Your seeds are not growing," he said.

Wóiki turned and looked down the rows he had made. "I am not worried. In a short time those plants will be sprouting." But Wóiki, who had eaten every seed Ijlió had given to him, was now sick to his stomach.

By the time Ijlió reached the end of a row,
the plants behind him had already sprouted.

"Are you feeling sick?" Ijlió asked when he noticed that Wóiki held his stomach and looked pale.

"No, why should I be?" replied Wóiki as he lay down and groaned. "I just need to rest for a while." In a short time Wóiki fell into a fitful sleep.

As Wóiki slept, Ijlió continued to plant his garden. By the time Wóiki awoke, Ijlió's garden was complete. The crops in the first rows he had set into the earth had grown so tall that flowers were already forming on them.

"You seem to have eaten something that gave you indigestion," said Ijlió.

"Oh no," Wóiki protested, "I was just a little tired, that's all."

"Because of your laziness, you are now going to have to work very hard to get food from your garden," said Ijlió. "No longer will seeds grow and produce a crop of fruit and vegetables as soon as they are planted. You will have to water and weed them. You must wait for many weeks and months before your crops mature for the harvest. Some of the seeds you plant will sprout and produce, and some will not."

The Elders say that, because human beings took after Wóiki instead of Ijlió, this is the way it has been in all of our gardens ever since.

The Coming of Seeds & Gardens

An Elfin Harvest

In the lovely land of Seim, there once was a farm that stretched for miles in every direction. The farmer was proud to own such rich cropland, which had been well tended by his family for generations. He worked long days to produce the best crop the soil could grow. Plowing and planting was hard work, but the harvest was the most difficult of all. In those days, there were few people who could come help cut the grain, tie it into sheaves and bring it into the barn. In some years, when the crop could not be harvested before the frost arrived, some of the grain was lost.

One year, when the grain had ripened, and the sun arched low in the southern sky, there came many weeks of cool, rainy days. "What are we going to do?" the farmer asked his wife. "I cannot begin the harvest until the sky clears."

"We must be patient," she replied. "Remember what my papa used to say, 'Never is help closer than in your time of greatest need.'"

At last, one morning, the sun shone in a clear sky. A golden sea of grain rippled at the hand of the morning breezes. The farmer went out for a walk in the fields. Even though he stood in the midst of breathtaking beauty, he was worried to the point of fear. "What am I to do?" he cried aloud. "All this bounty and no way to bring in the harvest before the frost comes."

"Fear not," came a reply as if Earth itself was speaking. "You shall have the help you need."

"Who torments me with such promises?" asked the farmer.

"It is we," came the reply. "Fulfill our wishes and your grain will soon be cut."

Then the farmer realized that it was the elves speaking. When they had made their wishes clear, he rushed through the field and into the kitchen. As quickly as they could, the farmer and his wife made a giant pot of stew and set it out in the middle of the parlor, arranging the room as they would when expecting the best company. Next to the pot of stew, they placed another pot that was just as large, but upside down. When all was ready, the couple went into the next room and closed the door all but a crack.

They peered into the parlor and waited all day, but nothing happened. Finally, when the crescent moon hung amber in the starry sky, the patter of

Tiny elves swung their silver scythes and the grain fell before them.

many feet came down the road. Out in the field, hundreds of tiny elves swung their silver scythes and the grain fell before them. They sang a song as they worked:

> *Your fields of grain will soon be shorn,*
> *we'll work all night, until the morn.*
> *But if you want the sheaves to take,*
> *beware, for knots we cannot make.*

Well before the moon had set, the waves of grain that once blanketed the surrounding hills had fallen under the swift blades of the elfin scythes. When the last stroke had been made, there came a shuffling of many tiny feet into the parlor. The hardworking elves had soon eaten their fill of the fine stew that had been set out for them. Even though the farmer, his wife and even the distant neighbors could hear the elves as they sang, danced and played their

103

An Elfin Harvest

tunes, the people were forbidden from looking into the parlor. When the sun broke over the hills of freshly cut grain, the celebration stopped as quickly as it had begun.

As the farmer and his wife crept into the parlor, they were awestruck. In place of the two pots, as a show of gratitude for the fine hospitality they had received, the elves had left an intricately carved wooden table decorated with every subtle color of Earth and Sky. The farmer and his wife invited all the neighbors to come visit and gaze upon the magnificent table.

All day the neighbors worked side by side with the farmer and his wife. By sunset, the grain had been tied into sheaves and brought into the barn. That night, the couple held a feast for the neighbors as thanks for the help that saved their crop.

To this day, generations hence, the table of the elves stands in that house. Many say that it has been preserved so well, and its magic is so strong, that the paint shines as fresh as dew upon the flower petals of springtime. The good folks of Seim say that ever since the elves' visit and the giving of the table, good fortune has prevailed throughout that land.

The elves in this story are sometimes called Haug-Folk, *which means "the hidden folk," "the unseen beings" or "the people of the mounds." They are similar to fairies.*

104

Lessons

See the "Activities" section for ideas on how to explore these lessons.

The Bay-Tree Girl is about a young woman whose beauty is inspired by the black berries of the tufted bay tree, whose love for the prince embraces like waves upon the shore. This Greek story reveals that there is a strong connection between people and trees, which have powerful healing qualities. We learn of the importance of faith, honesty and loyalty in a loving relationship. The number forty is significant at the end of the story.

In **Kospi & the First Flowers,** the Tehuelche Indians explain how flowers came into the world. There is a strong connection between flowers and water. The first flowers grow following a time of storms, when ice melts, rain falls and lightning strikes. The beauty of these flowers comes from the fair young woman named Kospi.

This mysterious story from Vietnam, **Befriended by Flowers,** comes to us as softly as a warm spring breeze. The young man, Hà Nhân Giã, makes friends with two beautiful, joyful young women. But things are not what they appear to be. The young women are the spirits of rare flowers. Hà Nhân Giã holds a ceremony to put the spirits at rest and bring them peace. Rare flowers need special care. There is a strong connection between flowers, youth, poetry, beauty and the pleasures of the senses.

In **The Coming of Seeds & Gardens,** Wuéla, the Moon, gives Ijlió, the Armadillo, the first garden seeds. These crops grow and can be harvested soon after planting. Wuéla shows Ijlió how to gather food from wild plants, and says to leave food on the plants for the future. But Wóiki, the Fox, the impatient trickster, eats his seeds instead of planting them. In this Chorote story, people take after Wóiki, so we have to work hard to grow our gardens and wait months to harvest. Because of Wóiki, some seeds sprout and some do not.

An Elfin Harvest reminds us that rich soil, hard work and a little luck are needed for successful farming. The farmer's ripe grain must be harvested quickly, so the elves offer to cut the fields in exchange for a hearty meal. Later, the neighbors bind the sheaves and bring them into the barn. This Scandinavian story teaches the virtue of cooperation. It shows that hard work is inspired by a generous reward of good food and celebration. The elves leave a beautifully carved wooden table for the farmer and his wife, whose faith is rewarded with a lasting gift far beyond their expectations.

Seven

Animals

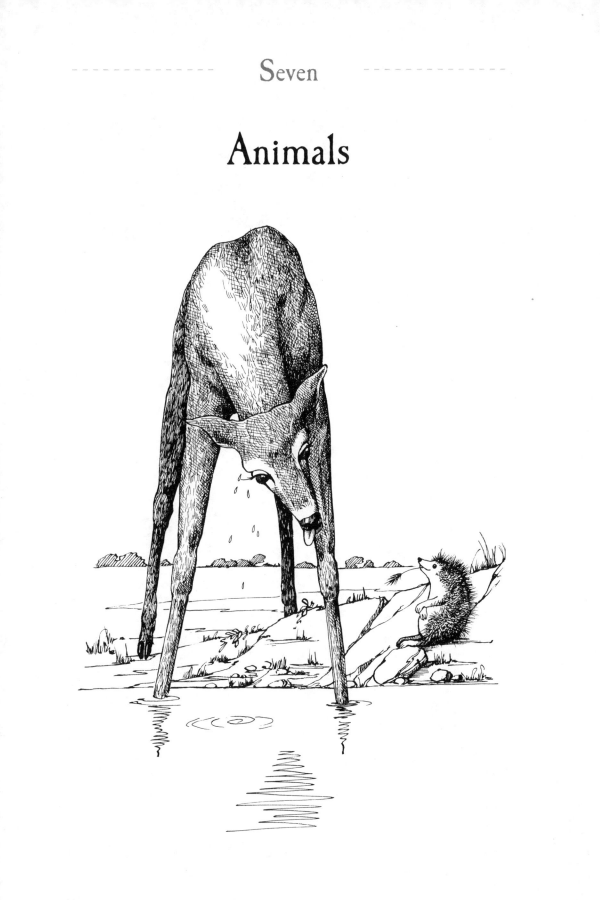

How Lion Lost
the Power of Flight

(South Africa)

Lion flapped great wings of skin and glided into his lair. *Oom Leeuw*, the Lion, folded the powerful wings back along his haunches. Angry at missing his prey, he strutted around the cave and beat the tips of his wings against the ground. "Tr-r-r-r," Oom Leeuw's growl shook the earth. As his voice rolled across the land, animals for miles around stopped whatever they were doing and looked up in fear.

With a great flapping that raised the dust and rattled the bones littering the floor of his cave, Oom Leeuw rose into the air. Once more he roared and set off to the south where game was plentiful. In the distance, Oom Leeuw saw a herd of springbok grazing the grasslands. He chose the most plump member of the herd, then Oom Leeuw folded his wings and dropped like an arrow from the sky. At the last moment, his iron claws gleaming in the sunlight, the lion fell upon the helpless animal.

Oom Leeuw flew with the springbok back to his lair. As he landed, the two crows who guarded the bones of his past meals hopped out of his way. These were not ordinary black crows—they were the rare white crows of which only one is born in many generations. Whenever a white crow hatches, it is given to Oom Leeuw as a future guardian of the bones. When the oldest white crow dies, the next eldest becomes the leader of the crows. Although the crows and all the other animals wondered why Oom Leeuw was afraid that something would happen to the bones of the animals he had eaten, no one was brave enough to ask him. The White Crows lived to make sure that none of the bones were ever broken.

One day, as Oom Leeuw was out hunting and the White Crows sat faithfully upon the bones, Bullfrog hopped into the door of the cave. "You White Crows," he asked, "why are you sitting here upon this pile of old bones?"

"We are the guardians of these bones," replied the White Crows. "It is our task to make sure that no harm comes to them while Oom Leeuw is away. These bones must never be broken."

"What a boring way to spend your days," said Bullfrog. "You have earned a break from this endless task. Fly out over the countryside and see what a beautiful day has dawned. I will stay here and make sure that these bones are safe."

With a great flapping, Oom Leeuw rose into the air.

They hopped to the door of Oom Leeuw's lair and carefully searched the sky. Oom Leeuw was nowhere to be seen. "Craw, craw," cried the White Crows as they flapped their wings and soared into the freedom of the open sky.

Bullfrog watched until the crows disappeared in the hazy blue. "Now is my chance to break these old bones. We will see what happens to Oom Leeuw when his precious bones are shattered." As Bullfrog hopped around the cave, the bones cracked, smashed and crunched with a sickening sound. When he was done, Bullfrog left the cave and hopped off toward the safety of the water that lay behind his dam.

The White Crows returned to the cave. In horror they found the rubble that was once a pile of old bones. Before Bullfrog reached his home, the White Crows flew toward him. "Craw, craw," they cried. "Why have you done such a terrible thing, Bullfrog? Oom Leeuw will kill us all with his iron claws."

Bullfrog ignored the White Crows and continued hopping. Once he reached the edge of the water, Bullfrog sat upon his dam and said, "I am not afraid of the terrible Oom Leeuw. When he comes home to find his old bones broken to bits, tell him old Bullfrog smashed his bones. Oom Leeuw knows where to find me."

The White Crows became so angry that they flew down to attack Bullfrog. But he leaped so quickly into the water that the White Crows found their beaks stuck in the mud upon which Bullfrog had been sitting. All that remained of Bullfrog was a ripple where he had entered the watery blue depths.

Out in the bush, Oom Leeuw was stalking his prey. He saw a zebra at the edge of a herd. Oom Leeuw leaped into the air and flapped his wings, but he fell back to the ground and found that he could not fly. Time and again Oom Leeuw tried to rise into the air, but each time he came crashing down to Earth.

"Rooo-rrr, rooo-rrr," cried Oom Leeuw until the ground shook and the trees swayed. Then there was a great silence as all the animals stopped to listen. But it was no use. Oom Leeuw could not fly. Quickly he ran along across the grasslands toward his lair.

When Oom Leeuw climbed, hot and tired, into the mouth of his cave, the White Crows cowered. But what was the great, powerful Oom Leeuw doing walking home under the hot, midday sun? "Look what you have done!" roared the lion. "You foolish crows, the bones are broken and I can no longer fly! I am going to eat you!"

When the crows saw that Oom Leeuw had lost his power of flight, they were no longer afraid. The two white birds circled the great lion's head and taunted him with their cries. "Too bad for the great Ooomy," they said. "He cannot catch us without his wings of skin. We are going to tell all the other animals what has happened."

Over and over Oom Leeuw leaped up and clawed at the swooping crows. But it was no use. At last, he lay panting upon the pile of broken bones.

"We did not break your old bones, but the one who did says he is not afraid of Oom Leeuw," screamed the White Crows. "He said that Oom Leeuw can find him at his dam." Then the crows swooped down one last time, pecked the lion on his head and flew off.

Oom Leeuw rose to his feet. He walked slowly toward the home of Bullfrog and saw him sunning on his dam. Quietly, the lion crept up behind Bullfrog and lunged. Bullfrog cried "Ho!" as he leaped off his dam. Oom Leeuw caught only a mouthful of mud. Bullfrog swam underwater and came up on the opposite shore of the pond. Oom Leeuw looked up to see Bullfrog sitting and calmly blinking his eyes from across the pond. Again and again Oom Leeuw sprang after the quick-legged frog. Over and over Bullfrog yelled "Ho!" leaped into the water and appeared on the opposite shore.

At last, Oom Leeuw realized that he would never catch Bullfrog. The downhearted lion walked home and tried unsuccessfully to repair the broken bones that littered the floor of his cave.

How Lion Lost the Power of Flight

Since that day, Oom Leeuw has never flown. He no longer has wings and has learned how to hunt by quietly sneaking up on his prey, rushing up and catching them in his iron claws. Again the animals have learned to fear the great lion.

Although the White Crows can still be seen, they have lost their power of speech. "Craw, craw, craw" is all they can say. Bullfrog lives in that same pond and suns himself upon the dam. As soon as Oom Leeuw, some other animal or a human being comes along, Bullfrog leaps up, cries "Ho!" and disappears into the safe, blue waters.

Abu l'Hssein, the Generous

Arab
(EGYPT)

ABU L'HSSEIN, THE FOX, was trotting along a trail one day when he saw Raven perched in a tree. "Friend, Raven," called Abu l'Hssein, "would you like to come and visit me? I will give you something good to eat."

"Yes, I would like that," replied Raven.

"Meet me at the rock in front of my den this evening," said Abu l'Hssein as he loped toward home. Once he arrived at his den, Abu l'Hssein began to prepare a meal of porridge for Raven. First he put some camel's milk in a pot and boiled it slowly over the fire. When the milk was ready, he mixed in some flour and stirred until it thickened.

Raven soon flew in and landed near Abu l'Hssein.

"Hello," said Abu l'Hssein.

"What are you making?" asked Raven.

"Dinner," replied Abu l'Hssein. Raven, who was very hungry, watched as his friend prepared the meal.

Once the porridge was done, Abu l'Hssein poured it out onto the flat rock on which he was standing. "Here is our meal," he said. "Eat well, my friend."

Raven pecked and pecked at the porridge, but was barely able to eat a tiny morsel. The longer he tried, the more frustrated and hungry he became. Meanwhile, Abu l'Hssein lapped up the porridge until his belly was full.

"This foolish Abu l'Hssein," thought Raven, "what kind of friend is he? I cannot eat this way!"

"Abu l'Hssein," said Raven in the most friendly manner he could manage, "you have been most kind and generous by inviting me for this fine meal. Please allow me to repay the favor and prepare a feast for you. I will provide as many sweet dates as you can possibly eat!"

Since sweet dates were Abu l'Hssein's favorite food, he became very excited. "Absolutely!" he cried. "Those dates grow so high in the date palms that I can only eat the few that fall on the ground and don't get consumed before I happen to find them."

"Excellent," answered Raven. "Meet me at the base of my tree tomorrow at sunset." Raven then flew toward home.

113

Raven wrapped his wings around his middle and groaned with delight.

Abu l'Hssein arrived the following evening just as the sun was dipping below the distant hills. He saw his friend, Raven, up in the date palm tree, silhouetted against the orange glow of a beautiful evening sky.

"I am going to knock these dates down for you to eat," Raven called down to Abu l'Hssein. "Get ready to catch them." Raven started picking the sweet dates. But, instead of knocking them down where Abu l'Hssein could reach them, he dropped them into the middle of a dense thorn bush.

Abu l'Hssein ran in circles around the thorn bush in search of a way in. But, no matter how hard he tried, Abu l'Hssein could not reach through the thorns to get the dates. In a short time his snout was cut up, his lips were red and swollen and his paws were raw and bleeding from reaching into the thorns.

Raven flew down from the tree. He used his hard beak and scaly claws to pluck one date after another from amid the dense thorns. Soon, he had eaten his fill. Raven sat back against the base of the date palm, wrapped his wings around his middle and groaned with delight.

At that moment, Abu l'Hssein realized what Raven had been doing. Instead of looking upon his friend as an inferior, Abu l'Hssein now regarded Raven as an equal. Abu l'Hssein had developed a deep respect for his friend. He realized that, although Raven's ways were different than his own, they worked just as well to help him survive.

Mighty Tiger & the Hare

Hui
(CHINA)

TIGER STALKED HIS PREY around the steep slopes of his mountain home. He had no reason to fear any other animal. Even the human beings were afraid of Tiger, who would attack a person if he was hungry enough.

"Allah has made me the mightiest animal," boasted Tiger. "He has given me permission to eat all the others. Wherever I go, the animals tremble with fear and flee for their lives!"

Still, Tiger had to work hard to catch his prey. "There must be an easier way for me to catch my food," said Tiger. "One day I will be old, and I will not be able to run as swiftly."

Tiger's mind was working as he walked across the grasslands and into the edge of the forest at the base of his mountain. "Ahh," said Tiger to himself at last, "that is a plan that will work. It will work because the animals cannot escape me and must do as I say."

"Come, gather 'round," Tiger roared to the other animals from atop his mountain. Slowly, the animals crawled, hopped, flew, walked and slithered into the clearing where Tiger was standing.

"None of you is as strong or swift as I am," said Tiger. "You can never escape me. You have no choice but to do whatever I tell you. And, because I grow bored eating the same thing every day, this is what you are going to do. Each morning, one of you will come to my lair. Every day, a different kind of animal will present itself. When you arrive on the appointed day, you will be my breakfast."

"Never!" cried the animals. "You will have to chase us and catch us as you always have."

"Very well," said Tiger. "If you try to deceive me, or if you do not come when it is your turn, I will search until I find you. Then, you, and all those like you, will be eaten."

"How will we know when it is our turn?" asked the animals, who knew that it was no use to defy Tiger's wishes.

"That, I will leave up to you," Tiger replied.

"Why don't we start with the largest animals first," suggested Hare, who knew the he was one of the smallest. "Then we can work our way down in size." The other animals glared at Hare for suggesting such a thing.

"Excellent idea!" Tiger agreed. "And don't forget what will happen if you do not show up when it is your turn!"

Many days, weeks and months passed and the larger animals took turns presenting themselves to Tiger for breakfast. But, because his meals were getting smaller and smaller, Tiger's hunger was growing. He anxiously awaited the arrival of his breakfast each day.

Finally, the day arrived when Hare was required to present himself to Tiger. The sun poked its head up above the trees in the east, but there was no sign of Hare. Higher in the sky rose the sun, but Hare did not come. Tiger grew ever more hungry and impatient. Finally, as the day wore on, Hare ambled slowly up the trail.

"You are late! Where have you been?" roared Tiger in a voice that bent the trees and caused Hare to tumble backward, head over paws.

"Something terrible has happened," Hare exclaimed. "A tiger even more powerful than you has captured my wife, and I am sure she is about to be eaten. Please help me, or you will have no young hares to eat when she is gone."

"What!" screamed Tiger. "Where has this tiger come from?"

"I do not know, most powerful one," answered Hare.

"Roorrh!" bellowed Tiger in a voice that shook the ground. "Where is this tiger now?"

"It is waiting for you at the spring even as we speak. I last saw him there," said Hare as he pointed up the trail he had come by.

"Show me where he is," demanded Tiger.

Hare led Tiger down the narrow trail that he used to find his way around the mountainside.

"Oh, Great One," said Hare respectfully, "the other tiger may be laying a trap. He could jump out from behind a bush and eat me at any time. Then you would have no meal and no one to show you where you might find him."

"What would you have me do?" asked Tiger.

"Perhaps, if you carry me gently in your mouth, I will be safe."

At that, Tiger carefully picked Hare up and held him in his great jaws. Hare was now more terrified than he had ever been in his life, but he began to whistle so that Tiger would not suspect.

After a good distance, they came to a large spring of crystal clear water.

116 "In there!" screamed Hare, "that is where you will find the other tiger who is holding my wife in his mouth!"

Tiger peered over the edge of the shoreline and saw another tiger that was also carrying a hare in its mouth.

"Roorrh!" cried Tiger. In his anger, Tiger dropped Hare and dove at the tiger in the spring. Hare danced up and down on the bank as he watched

*Tiger peered over the edge of the shoreline and saw another tiger
that was also carrying a hare in its mouth.*

Tiger in his fury, searching frantically underwater for the other tiger with the
hare in its mouth. Tiger was so determined to defeat his enemy that he stayed
under too long and drowned.

Hare laughed as he turned away from the spring in which Tiger had met
his end. "I guess there wasn't enough room on this mountain for both of us
tigers after all," said Hare as he hopped homeward toward his wife and family.
From that day forward, Hare, and all the animals who lived on that mountain,
lived long, contented lives.

Mighty Tiger & the Hare

The First Bats

Jakaltec–Maya
(Guatemala and Mexico)

Soon after the animals were made, the Creator showed each kind where and how it was going to live. The birds were most pleased. They could fly, sing beautiful songs and construct fine nests. *Tx'ow*, Mouse, however, was envious as she watched the birds in their free flight.

"What are you waiting for?" asked the Creator. "Start living. You can eat beans, corn and many other seeds. You are so close to the ground, and your mouth is so small that you can find and eat food that others overlook."

Tx'ow was stubborn. She just stood there.

"Go!" said the Creator as he grabbed Tx'ow's tail and flung her into a field. Tx'ow stayed right where she landed, watching the birds and wishing she could do more than simply hop around.

"Perhaps," thought Tx'ow, "if I convince all the mice how wonderful it would be to fly, the Creator will listen to us." After visiting all her relations and arguing her case, Tx'ow returned to the Creator followed by a horde of mice.

"Yes, what is it?" demanded the Creator of the impressive group of mice.

"Squeet'zi, squeet'zi, squeet'zi," came the response.

"You desire the power of flight, as I have given the birds, is that not so?" asked the Creator.

All the mice answered at once in a loud voice, "Squeet'zi, squeet'zi, squeet'zi!"

"Then this is what you must do," said the Creator. "Meet me at sunrise where there is a great canyon called *Tx'eqwob'al,* the Jumping Place."

So excited were the mice that they feasted late into the night. "This way," they thought, "we will be well fed and strong in the morning."

The first rays of sun shone upon the Creator, who waited at the edge of the chasm. Soon appeared the largest group of mice that had ever gathered.

"It is time," said the Creator. The mice began to chatter.

"Anyone who can jump across this ravine and land safely on the other side will be given wings and the power of flight."

One at a time, the mice ran to the edge of the chasm and leaped into the air. Many fell short and remained mice thereafter. Those who reached the other side grew thin wings of skin. Their tails fell off and the tiny claws grew long and curved. They flew away and began a life amid the dark caves in the mountains.

Those who reached the other side grew thin wings of skin.

When all of the mice had jumped, the Creator spoke to them one last time. "Now it is done. Those of you who are still mice will eat seeds and nuts. You can make warm nests and finish them with a soft lining. You can nest in the trees or wherever you find a good space for a home. From this day forth, the rest of you will now be known as *Sotz'*, the bats. The mouse's night will be your day. Some of you will eat mosquitoes, others will eat fruit and still others will drink blood. No longer will you live in cozy nests. By your sharp claws you will cling upside down from the roofs of caverns, *nchach'en*.

The mouse, Tx'ow, saw that Sotz', the bats, too, were not entirely pleased with their lives. That is how mice came to be content with the gifts they received when first created.

The First Bats

119

Hedgehog Races Deer

(Germany)

Hedgehog and deer sat along the banks of a pond.

"I have the most remarkable fur of any animal," said Hedgehog. "Once I roll up into a ball, no one can harm me."

"Look at my magnificent ears," said Deer. "No one can match them. With these ears, I can hear better than any other animal."

On they continued for some time, bragging about who was the smartest, strongest and most handsome.

"No matter what you may or may not be good at, or well built for," said Deer smartly, "there is no denying that I am the fastest. Why, those little stubs that carry you along can hardly be called legs. They don't even keep your belly off the ground!"

"You are jealous," replied Hedgehog. "Your legs are so long they get tangled beneath you and cause you to stumble. I could run the length of these woods, swim across the river and sprint up to the top of the hill before you even had a chance to get those spider legs working together."

"Very well," said Deer as he raised his ears erect, "now we will see who is telling the truth. Words are one thing, but deeds tell the story."

"If I am to run the best race I can, I am going to need to walk the route to see where the rocks and branches are, and to count the number of paces I must go to reach the hilltop. That way, I will know how to pace myself," said Hedgehog.

"That sounds reasonable enough," Deer agreed. "We will meet here tomorrow at sunrise to begin the race." Deer went home to his yard, laughing at the foolish Hedgehog.

The next morning, Hedgehog met Deer at the starting line. "Let's go," said Deer, who stomped his hooves, cried "Holla" and ran off. "I will not even have to exert myself," thought Deer. "That dim-witted Hedgehog will never keep up."

About midmorning, Deer stopped at a small stream along the trail. After taking a nice, long drink, he sat down against the base of a tree for a brief rest.

"Don't tell me you are tired already!" cried a voice from the underbrush.

"What? Who?" cried Deer. Then he saw it was Hedgehog speaking, who looked as fresh as when he had started the race.

There sat hedgehog, reclined along the riverbank.
"Oh, I've been here for quite a while," he said.

"Well, of course I'm not tired," said Deer, who really had been out of breath when he first stopped. "It's just that I'm so much faster than you that I can afford to rest now and then without falling behind."

"Don't rest too long, my friend," said Hedgehog as he ambled down the trail. At that, Deer jumped to his feet and huffed past Hedgehog, running as fast as he could but trying to look like he was not exerting himself. All the while, Deer was thinking, "Just my luck to race the fastest Hedgehog in the world!"

Hedgehog Races Deer

Throughout the day, wherever Deer stopped to rest, to his disbelief, Hedgehog was already waiting there for him. Each time he left a resting spot, Deer tried to run a bit faster to put Hedgehog behind him. As the day wore on, Deer's tongue hung further and further out of his mouth, and his nose turned from pink to red.

By midafternoon, Deer came to the edge of the forest. In this place there was a lovely field of wildflowers that reached down to the riverbank. It was a favorite drinking and resting place of the animals. "Now, I can finally stop for a while before I begin climbing the hillside," thought Deer. Then he screamed, "Ahh! How did you get here, Hedgehog?" There sat Hedgehog, reclined along the riverbank, chewing the end of a stalk of grass in his mouth.

"Oh, I've been here for quite a while. Did you ever notice how many different flowers bloom along this river? Don't tell me you are just now arriving?"

"Well … I … uh … why no, I have been here for a long time, scouting up and down the riverbank for the best place to swim across," said Deer.

"Yes, I did the same thing," replied Hedgehog. "This is the spot right here." Hedgehog jumped into the river and started to swim across.

Deer, who was as flustered as he had ever been, jumped in and made his way across while both swimming and drinking to save time. He swam right past Hedgehog, climbed up onto the opposite bank, shook himself off and hobbled up the trail toward the top of the hill.

Gasping, fumbling and crawling his way up the steep slope on his knees, Deer's heart felt like it was going to burst. He had been at a full run for most of the day, without a moment's rest. Just as he came over the ridge and could see the large boulder that crowned the hill, Deer drew back in shock. There, sitting on top of the hill, was Hedgehog.

"Sorry, Deer, I guess the distance was just too much for you, eh?"

At that moment, Deer grabbed at his chest, gasped and fell over. He was panting harder than he ever had. Spitting and wheezing, his tongue drooping from the side of his mouth, Deer barely managed to say, "Hedgehog, you have won. You are indeed the fastest among the animals."

Deer never noticed that he had really been meeting up with many different hedgehogs as he raced along. They were the brothers, sisters and cousins of the Hedgehog he had challenged, and each one looked exactly like all of the others.

122   *Many race stories are similar to this story of "Hedgehog Races Deer." There is a Bondei (Africa) story of "The Tortoise and the Falcon," a South African story of "Steenbuck and Tortoise," an Apinaye (Brazil) story of "The Deer and the Turtle," a Seneca (United States) story of "Turtle Races with Bear," a Guajiro (Venezuela and Colombia) story of "The Dog and the Jaguar" and several Japanese stories of "The Whale and the Sea Slug," "The Fox and Crayfish" and "The Mudsnail and the Fox."*

Whither the Animals' Freedom?

(POLAND)

AT ONE TIME, ALL OF THE ANIMALS WERE FREE, proud and happy. They all lived well together. Not one animal answered to the wishes, or did the bidding, of human beings. There were no barns or fences, saddles or whips. The cat was the only animal who listened at doorway and windowsill for news from the world of people. She liked to boast and tell the other animals that she knew much more than them.

The freedom of each kind of animal rested with a beautiful parchment scroll, on which was recorded all known history of that animal down through the generations. Every scroll bore a wax seal and was tied with silk. If anything were to happen to a scroll, or if it should be lost, that group of animals would forever lose both its history and freedom.

"We should take good care of our parchments," said Horse one day. "We need to put them in a safe, guarded place watched over by someone whom we trust." The animals debated. Who would prove to be the best protector of the precious scrolls?

"I think Cat would make a good sentry for our parchments," Dog said at last. "She likes to lie about, but is always alert. Cat knows more about human beings than any other animal. She could use that knowledge to keep our parchments safe from them."

All the animals looked at one another. Although they did not like Cat's closeness to people, Dog's ideas made sense.

"Would you watch over the animals' parchments?" they asked Cat.

"Well, perhaps I might be interested. Let me think it over," said Cat coolly.

At that, many animals began to plead with Cat, but she acted coy. At last, the animals said, "We will give you three days to consider."

Three days later, the animals called another meeting and Cat accepted the responsibility as watcher of the scrolls. Many animals brought their parchments to Cat for safekeeping, including Goat, Horse, Chicken, Wolf, Cow, Sheep and Ox.

"I know an excellent place to keep these parchments," said Cat as she carried them away by the pawful. Cat took the scrolls to a quiet, dusty corner of an attic in a house where a man lived alone. "No one ever disturbs this chest," she said to herself as she laid the scrolls inside. Cat closed the lid tightly. Over the

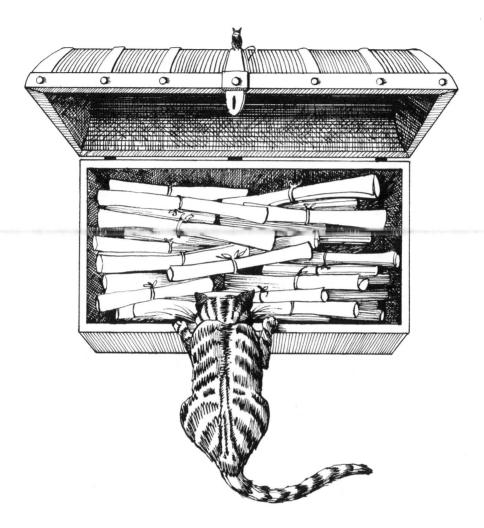

"No one ever disturbs this chest," Cat said to herself
as she laid the scrolls inside.

coming months, Cat checked on the scrolls two or three times and found that they were keeping well. Then she forgot them.

One year passed and the animals held a gathering to discuss the scrolls. "How are things going?" they asked Cat. "Are our scrolls safe and in one piece?"

"The last time I saw them they looked just as they had when I took them from you last year," said Cat.

"Why don't we take a peek," said Wolf.

That night, several of the animals crept up into the man's attic and found the chest. A cloud of dust rose from the chest as Wolf opened the lid. When Wolf peered inside, he saw several piles of old seeds and scraps of dry, brittle paper that lay in heaps at the bottom of the chest.

"We are done for!" whispered Wolf in horror. "Mice have destroyed all of our family parchments!" As soon as she heard that, Cat let out a shrill "Raaoow!" She leaped out of the window and escaped along the top of a nearby roof.

"You fool!" Wolf bellowed to Dog as anger welled up inside. Then he bared his white fangs. "Why did you ever suggest the Cat?!" Dog then ran away and hid under the man's bed.

"First the Cat," said the man, "now the Dog. Soon all the animals will be at my service." When he found Wolf in his attic, the man grabbed his gun and chased Wolf into the forest. Wolf was so enraged that he began to pursue and attack any animal he could find. Other animals saw Wolf acting that way and began to do the same, including Fox, Lynx and Marten.

On that night the animals lost their ability to live well together. Moreover, many of them lost their freedom. Some, such as Sheep, Goat, Horse, Ox and Pig, became so afraid to live in the wild that they took refuge in the shelters built by human beings. The more barns and stables that people built, the more animals came to fill them. In order to earn their food, water and care, the animals were pressed into services that would have been beneath their dignity when they were free.

Because Dog had suggested Cat as the guardian of the scrolls, and Cat had failed in her duty, Dog was vengeful. Dog and Cat became especially bitter enemies. To this day, Cat blames the mice for chewing up the scrolls and has taken it out on that gentle race of animals ever since.

In this way, the destruction of the animals' parchment scrolls began a cycle of anger and revenge between many families of animals that has been carried down through the generations.

125

Lessons

See the "Activities" section for ideas on how to explore these lessons.

In the South African story, **How Lion Lost the Power of Flight,** Oom Leeuw, the lion, is a predator with wings, sharp claws and teeth. He loses his ability to fly when the irresponsible White Crows leave the lair unguarded. Then, the crows and Bullfrog take advantage of the lion. Bullfrog's speed, size and wit beat Lion's power and might. We learn how crows and bullfrogs live and why lions hunt the way they do today.

Abu l'Hssein, the Generous is really the selfish Fox. He offers Raven a meal that he knows Raven cannot eat. Raven returns the favor. In this humorous story from Egypt, we learn that each animal has its own, unique adaptations that allow it to survive. Abu l'Hssein discovers that what we do to others will also be done to us.

This Hui tale from China, **Mighty Tiger & the Hare,** shows how the powerful Hui can control the weak. Because he is lazy, Tiger forces all the other animals to come to him so he may eat them. Tiger feels invincible and will not tolerate the threat presented by a more powerful tiger, which Hare says has arrived on the mountain. In the end, Hare tricks Tiger and defeats the great cat. Tiger's own conceit is fatal when turned against himself.

In the Jakaltec-Maya story, **The First Bats,** these flying mammals come from unhappy mice who want to fly like birds. In truth, bats are not flying mice, they are a distinct order of mammals, *Chiroptera*, which means "hand wing." Those mice who grow wings and turn into flying bats discover that bats' lives are not perfect either. In this story, the remaining mice learn to be satisfied with who they are and how they live.

Hedgehog Races Deer is a silly tale from Germany about Deer, who cannot resist the chance to humiliate Hedgehog by beating him in a race. By tricking the Deer and winning the race, Hedgehog proves that competition is a test of physical skill and ability as well as a contest of wits. Hedgehog *does,* however, get away with cheating.

In **Whither the Animals' Freedom?** we learn that all animals were once wild, free and content, and that they got along well with each other. This story from Poland explains how the animals lost their freedom when the mice ate their parchment scrolls. Because they blame each other, the animals no longer get along. Many animals now live in buildings and do the bidding of their human masters.

Eight

Circle of Life

First People:
Children of the Macaques

Lisu

(CHINA)

MUBUPA FASHIONED EARTH FROM THE CLAY OF HEAVEN. The hills and valleys, rivers, lakes and oceans were the face of Earth looking up to Heaven in her joy at being alive.

"Now it is time to create the human beings," said the god Mubupa. "I will fashion them out of the mud from which I made Earth."

Mubupa took the mud and formed two macaque monkeys. He created trees and other plants so the macaques would have food, a home and places on which to climb. These contented macaques became the first human beings; the parents of all people who were yet to come.

The Macaque family spent many hours gathering food in the treetops. One day, when their son was still young enough to be nursing, the family went out to forage fruit and nuts. As Mother Macaque was eating, the hot sun beat down on the head of her son. Soon, he began to cry. His mother tried nursing him, but he continued to cry. She brought him into the shade of their house and tried to soothe him to sleep, but his cries grew into wails. Finally, Mother Macaque took her son to a shady place outdoors beneath the green umbrella of leaves. Here, she nestled him into a cradle made of boughs.

"There, there," said Mother Macaque. "Quiet now. It is time to sleep." Back and forth, the wind gently rocked the child. At last, his eyelids drooped as he settled into a deep slumber.

High in the treetop above the sleeping baby monkey, a parrot landed on a branch and began to pick at a pinecone to remove the seeds. After it had finished eating all of the pine nuts, the parrot dropped the heavy cone. Down, down it fell. At last, the pinecone struck the sleeping baby in the temple.

Mother Macaque bent over her child to see if he was all right. When she saw that he was no longer breathing, her cry of grief rang through the stillness of the forest.

"My child!" she cried. "What will I do without you? Others will have their children, but not I!" Louder, still, became her cries. Earth itself began to rumble, and quakes rocked the land. Lightning struck and thunder cracked over the forested valley below. Black clouds rolled across the face of the sun and a gloom settled over Earth.

Back and forth, the wind gently rocked the child.

"This is how it will be," cried Mother Macaque in a voice that caused all of the forest creatures to tremble. "All living things will come to an end. Trees will grow, then topple back into the soil. The seeds of new plants will grow from the life of old. People will not live forever. Everyone will die when it is their time. In this way, there will be a place on Earth for the children to come."

This is how birth and death came into the world. It has been that way ever since.

Death Becomes Final

Caduveo
(BRAZIL)

ONCE THERE WAS A TIME when death did not last. Death was a kind of sleep from which people would awake after two days had passed. That is how *Gô-noêno-hôdi*, the Creator, had made the world.

"This is not the way it should be," said *Caracará*, the Creator's companion. "There is only so much space on Earth. How can Earth feed everyone if no one dies, if everyone lives forever? In time there will be so many people that we will run out of food and Earth will be destroyed."

"There is much truth to what you are saying," Gô-noêno-hôdi agreed. "From this time on, whenever someone dies, they will not be revived in two days. They will remain forever in the slumber of death."

After some time had passed, Caracará's elderly mother died. He loved his mother very much. Heartbroken, Caracará visited Gô-noêno-hôdi and implored him to bring his mother back to life. With tears in his eyes he said, "Please, don't allow her to remain dead forever."

"If you would revive your mother," said Gô-noêno-hôdi, "you need only gather one of the common red lilies that grows in the marsh. Bring the flower to her grave, and wrap her hands around its smooth stem. Pull your mother up by this stem and she will come back to life."

Caracará rushed down to the marsh and found one of the red lilies growing there. It was a beautiful flower with many crimson petals that seemed to reach out and embrace the air above it. Caracará picked one of the blooms, being careful to leave it attached to the long, smooth stem.

When he arrived at the side of his mother's grave, he placed the stem of the red lily firmly in her hands. As Caracará pulled, his mother's hands began to rise. Then, the fragile stem broke. Caracará began to cry and rushed to Gô-noêno-hôdi's side.

"Gô-noêno-hôdi," sobbed Caracará, "the stem of the red lily broke as my mother held it in her hands and I tried to pull her up by it. The stem is not strong enough. Is there no other way that she can be brought back to life?"

"I am sorry," Gô-noêno-hôdi replied. "Your mother cannot be revived from the eternal sleep of death. There is nothing else you can do." To this day, death is a final state. No one comes back to life.

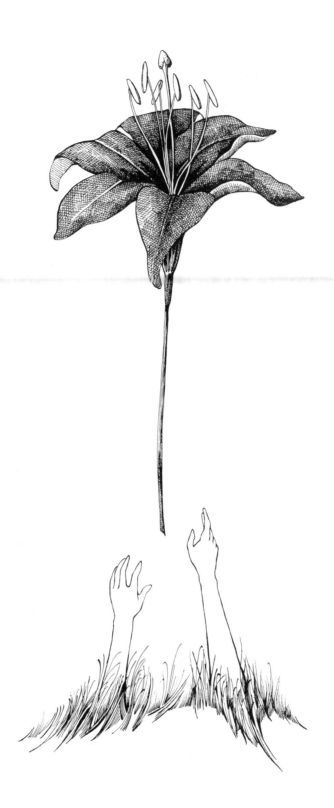

As Caracará pulled on the stem of the red lily, his mother's hands began to rise.

Magpie & the Bird Nests

(England)

Back when the animals were first learning how to live, Blackbird came to visit Magpie.

"What are you building?" asked Blackbird.

"I am making my nest," replied Magpie.

"What is a nest for?"

"It is a place in which to raise my young," replied Magpie.

Blackbird flew throughout the forests, fields and marshes. "Come and see the magnificent nest that Magpie is making," she told the other birds. Soon, they were all gathered in the branches, watching Magpie build her nest.

First, Magpie went to the shore of the pond and gathered some mud. She began to fashion this into a small bowl.

"Now I see how a nest is made," said Thrush, who flew off to build a nest of her own. To this day, Thrush uses mud to make her nest.

Then, Magpie went from bush to bush, gathered small sticks and wove them into the mud nest.

"I think this is a very clever nest in which to live," exclaimed Blackbird. She flew off and has since made her nest of mud and twigs.

Magpie made many more trips to the pond, gathering bits of mud in her beak. At last, the nest was lined with an inner coating of mud.

"That will be much stronger for we birds who are bigger than some of the others," said Owl. She went back to her pine tree and fashioned a layered nest of mud, sticks and mud.

Magpie began to tire, but she felt that her nest needed some adornment. She flew down to the ground and gathered the smallest twigs she could find. With these, Magpie wove a covering for her nest.

"What a fine looking nest," said Sparrow. "I think it is finally completed." With that, Sparrow flitted home and built a nest of the same kind.

Magpie needed some rest. She cozied up in her nest for a little while but could not quite find a comfortable position. "I think the inside of the nest needs something soft," she explained to the birds who were still watching. With her beak, Magpie plucked some feathers from her own breast and used them to line the nest.

"Make two, Maggie, make twoooo," moaned Turtle Dove.

"Ah," said Starling, "that's the nest for me." Since that day, Starlings have made soft, cozy nests lined with feathers.

Each time Magpie fussed with her nest, adding a bit here, tweaking a little there, another bird flew off and built its nest according to what it had learned from Magpie. Only one bird waited patiently to see how the nest would look when it was complete.

"Make two, Maggie, make twoooo," moaned Turtle Dove. Again and again she called. Finally, Magpie could stand it no longer.

"One nest is quite enough," she said.

Again, Turtle Dove said, "Make two, Maggie, make twoooo."

"Why ever would I need two?" asked Magpie.

Without pausing, Turtle Dove repeated, "Make two, Maggie, make twoooo."

At wit's end, Magpie cried, "Make it yourself!" Then she flew as far from Turtle Dove as she could go. "No longer am I going to teach the other birds how to build a nest. They will have to figure it out for themselves."

To this day, each bird makes its own unique kind of nest. But none makes a nest as fine and complete as that of Magpie.

The Caprice of Heron & Crane

(Russia)

Heron and Crane lived far apart, in the distant reaches of a vast marsh. Each day they stalked the shallow water in search of crayfish, minnows and other creatures to eat.

"This is a good home," thought Heron. "There is always plenty of food, and I enjoy the flowers that blossom here. But, whenever I see a bee visiting a water lily, I think of the buzzing hive to which it will return with its nectar. I am reminded of how lonely my life is."

"Why am I not happy?" Crane wondered. "What more could I ask for? I have enough to eat and drink. There is wide open space in which to roam. But there must be something more."

Just then, Crane gazed off in the distance and saw Heron looking for food in her part of the marsh out on the edge of the horizon. "There is a graceful bird. She has lacy feathers and a long, curved neck. I have always thought much of Heron. This would be a good time for us to visit."

Crane walked for several miles before coming to the home of Heron. He stood up on a rock and could not see her anywhere. "Hello, Heron, are you here?" he called.

"Why, yes," Heron replied as she stepped out from behind a tall, thick growth of shrubs. "What is it that you desire?"

"Dear Heron, I have everything I could want in my marsh. But I am the only one who lives there. I picture you, too, fishing the waters and wading past the lilies."

"What are you saying?" asked Heron.

"I am not sure. Well, I guess … ."

"What?" demanded Heron.

"Will you marry me?" asked Crane.

"I am afraid that could not possibly be," replied Heron. "We are friends now and marriage is the source of many arguments. Besides, would there be enough food in your part of the marsh for the two of us, plus our children? I think not."

"But … ," Crane tried to say.

"Not only that, I think you have snipped feathers and scrawny legs."

"Would you marry me?" asked Crane.
"I am afraid that could not possibly be," replied Heron.

Crane said no more. He turned, head bowed, and flew off to his corner of the marsh.

As Heron saw him go, she felt a pang in her own heart. "Why did I treat him so? I cannot leave things this way. Crane was sincere and would make a good husband." With those thoughts, Heron quickly flew off toward Crane's marsh.

"I have thought it over," said Heron. "I would indeed be pleased to have you as my husband."

"You mock me," responded Crane rather angrily. "It is too late. I have vowed to remain alone in light of your refusal."

Weeping, Heron made for home. "What have I done," she sobbed shamefully. "His offer had been sincere, and now he is no longer interested in me."

After some time passed, and Crane recovered from his hurt, he once again began to long for Heron. "I had her here in my own home, wanting to become my wife," he lamented. "But, in my blindness, I turned her away." As he dwelled on these thoughts, Crane grew sad and restless.

Up Crane flew to his friend's side once more. "Please forgive me," he said. "In my grief I could not think clearly. I will be your husband. Do not leave me to live a life alone."

A crooked smile came to Heron's face. "Well, I see, Sir Sharp Beak! But surely you remember what I said when you first asked me to wed. It will never come to pass."

Crane croaked a hoarse note that rang out over the quiet marsh. Then, on bowed wings, he rose up and flew homeward.

As Heron watched her suitor fade into the distance, her heart was wracked with pain. Her life, like his, was uneventful and dull. She longed for his caring and companionship. Before she knew what she was doing, and without even thinking, she was winging her way to his side. When Heron landed, she opened up her heart to Crane and shared regrets at having turned him down again.

"Hmm, I am afraid it is too late," he said curtly. "I, too, have changed my mind."

And so the fickle Crane and Heron continue to live alone, wading through the reeds of the misty marsh.

137

Lessons

See the "Activities" section for ideas on how to explore these lessons.

This Lisu story from China, **First People: Children of the Macaques,** tells of the beginning of Earth and humankind. People come from a pair of macaque monkeys, which are made of clay, the same as Earth. Death comes and makes room for the children yet to be born. Mother Macaque's grief causes earthquakes, lightning and thunder. This story also introduces the nutrient cycle by which plants grow from soil, create new seeds, die and decay back into the soil that will grow new plants.

According to the Caduveo story, **Death Becomes Final,** people once came back to life two days after they died. Caracará realizes that, if everyone lived, Earth would see great hunger and destruction. Agreeing, the Creator, Gô-noêno-hôdi, makes it so that no one ever awakes from death. But, blinded by grief when his mother dies, Caracará tries, unsuccessfully, to bring the dead back to life.

Magpie & the Bird Nests, a humorous story from England, shows that we can learn by watching others. None of the impatient birds, however, except for Turtle Dove, observes Magpie long enough to learn how to make a nest like hers. Bird nests and nestlings are a springtime sign of rebirth. The perfectly round hollows of bird nests symbolize the turning of the seasons and the Circle of Life.

The bee at the beginning of the Russian story, **The Caprice of Heron & Crane,** is a symbol of family. It causes Heron to reflect on how lonely she is. Crane realizes that life is more than just surviving. But Heron is too fussy and fickle to accept Crane's marriage proposal. Then, after being turned down, Crane allows hurt feelings, grief and anger to get in the way. Next, Heron's vengeful feelings keep them apart. Finally, Crane again changes his mind. Because these two birds, who care so much for each other, cannot rise above their petty feelings, they never begin to dance in the Circle of Life. The story also raises some questions: What is a species? Could two different kinds of birds mate and raise a family?

Nine

Stewardship

Disappearing Flowers

Arab
(SYRIA)

A GREAT PALACE GARDEN ONCE GREW containing every kind of flower found in that land. In some places the king and queen raised flowers whose seeds had been presented to them by visitors from many different countries. These were arranged in neat, ordered beds that looked like tapestries of color when viewed from the upper windows of the palace. Beyond the formal gardens grew the countless native flowers that the couple had spent a lifetime cultivating. As in nature, these flowers thrived beyond the castle, stretching out into the countryside as far as the eye could see.

Among the flowers were irises and jasmines, delicate anemones and tall, brightly colored lilies. All manner of insects hummed and buzzed amid the colorful petals of infinite shapes and hues. Many rare blooms flourished. Rarest of them all was a flower that no longer grew anywhere outside the garden. Its scent wafted a great distance and attracted distant passersby. One sniff of these perfumed petals and the most weary heart was uplifted and filled with hope.

Each morning, the king and queen took a walk among the flowers. On one particular morning, they approached the patch of rarest blooms.

"Look here," exclaimed the queen. "One of these flowers has been plucked from its stem."

"Indeed," said the king, "but who would do such a thing? Our garden is closely watched. This could not have happened by day. Why would anyone sneak into our garden to steal flowers in the middle of the night?"

The king and queen had three sons, of whom they were very proud. That night, they asked one of their sons to stand watch in the garden to find out who the flower thief might be. A tent was raised near the patch of rare blooms, and in it was placed a comfortable bed. As soon as the sun set, the first prince settled down into the soft bedding, and his eyes became heavy. The next morning, when he awoke from a deep slumber, the prince found that one more of the rare blooms had been picked. The next night, the second prince also fell asleep during his watch. The king then spoke sternly with his third, youngest son.

"Tonight, when you watch for the thief, you are not to use a tent or a bed. You will sit upon the cold, damp ground and stay awake! If we do not soon discover who is stealing our flowers, they will be wiped out forever and will never be seen again, for this is the only patch that grows upon Earth."

Not only did the third prince do as his father asked, he also made a small cut on his forearm and kept by his side a cup of salted water. Whenever he began to feel sleep coming over him, he dabbed a bit of salt water on the cut and stung himself back to wakefulness. All night he waited. When the silver moon had traveled most of the way across the sky, the prince began to think the thief would not come that night.

Just then, the prince looked into the cup and saw rings begin to dance out from the edge of the water as the ground shook time and again. When the prince looked up, he saw a *Marid,* a huge and powerful monster. Although his arms began to shake, and sweat rolled down his brow, the prince tightened the grip on his sword. As the Marid reached down to pick one of the rarest flowers, he came so close that the prince could smell his foul breath. At just the right moment, the prince plunged his sword into the monster's hand and drove it in to the haft. In agony, the beast ran off howling into the night, blood gushing from the deep wound.

At daybreak, the three princes set off in pursuit of the Marid. They followed his trail of blood away from the palace. It led out of the walled city to the mouth of an old, abandoned well. In that place, where travelers once drank from a cool spring and watered their animals, there was now only a deep, dusty pit.

"I am the oldest among us," said the first prince, "so I should be the one to defeat this Marid." He tied a rope around his waist and asked his brothers to lower him into the well. When the light of his lantern caused a shadow to dance on the wall of the shaft, the prince yelled, "Pull me up! Quickly, pull me up!" He had cowered at the sight of his own shadow.

"Let me try," said the second prince. As they lowered him into the darkness, the blade of his sword struck against a stone lining the well. He thought it was the Marid coming after him and screamed, "Get me out of here, *Now!*" His brothers heaved on the rope and raised him from the well as fast as they could.

The last-born among them said, "I am going down on the rope. No matter what happens, pay no attention to what I say, just keep lowering me until I touch the bottom." Down, down his brothers let the prince slip into the abyss. At last, the rope slackened.

142

The youngest prince untied the noose from his waist and began to walk around. He kicked up clouds of dust on the old, dry well bottom. In the distance, the prince saw a faint light. As he approached the lit passageway, a roaring filled his ears. In a short time, he stood in a brightly lit marble arch that opened into a vast chamber. At the opposite end of the great room was a stone chair in which was seated a breathtakingly beautiful princess. The ugly Marid

The ugly Marid lay asleep with his enormous head in the Princess's lap.

lay asleep with his enormous head in her lap. His snoring echoed through the dank air.

As the prince walked quietly forward, he noticed that the princess wore a necklace strung with the rare flowers the Marid had stolen from the palace garden. The petals seemed lit with a pale, moonlike glow. When the princess saw the prince approaching, she carefully, silently motioned toward the giant's blood-covered sword lying by his side. The prince caught her eye and nodded his understanding.

Before he struck, the prince rattled his sword in its scabbard to wake the Marid. He was no coward and would not strike even so foul a creature while it slept. The hideous beast stirred and his eyes gleamed like pits of fire. At once, using the full strength of both arms, the prince swung his blade and severed the monster's head from its shoulders. It rolled along the cobble floor and smashed against the wall near the arching doorway, crumbling it into a pile of rubble.

"Thank you for ridding me of this horrible creature!" the princess said as she approached the prince. "He kidnapped me from my home and has kept me prisoner here for many days. But how are we going to escape? The only way to the surface is blocked by the broken stones in the doorway."

The prince and princess wandered down a passageway that led out into the Marid's underground garden. There an old man stepped out from behind an ancient tree. He was dressed in white and wore a turban of wisdom.

"Sir," called the princess, "how might we escape this place and return to our homes?"

"You will see a black ram and a white ram locked in combat. Ride the correct one and it will carry you home."

When the old man stepped back behind the wizened old tree, two rams emerged from the other side, violently butting horns as if trying to kill one another. The prince took the princess's hand and led her over to the white ram. "Quickly," he said grabbing onto its horns, "jump upon its back and ride with me." As soon as they climbed onto the back of the white ram, they found themselves standing at the mouth of the well where the prince's two brothers were waiting.

In time, the princess and the youngest prince were wed. From that day on, it is said, they wandered the countryside and became the guardians of the rarest flowers that grow.

Turtle Returns the Gift

(Japan)

Once there was a statesman named Fujiwara no Yamakage, and he had many children. Fujiwara loved his children with all his heart, especially his youngest son. The child was also deeply loved by his stepmother, who treated him with great kindness.

One day, a messenger knocked on Fujiwara's door. When the door swung open, the man proclaimed, "I have a message here for Master Yamakage."

"Please come in," said Fujiwara with a gesture. "What is your message?"

"It is contained in this letter," replied the messenger as he handed an envelope to Fujiwara.

Fujiwara opened the envelope and read. He smiled, thanked the messenger and saw him out the door. Then, Fujiwara gathered his family together. "I have good news," he said. "I have been appointed Viceroy of Kyushu. We are going on a great journey." Fujiwara's wife and children were very excited.

"When shall we leave?" asked the children.

"Tomorrow," replied their father.

The following morning, Fujiwara, his family and their entourage sailed for Kyushu. It was a long journey of many days. On the third day, the wind began to howl and whip the seas into a froth. Waves, which loomed like mountains above the small sailboats, began to break over the decks. Sails tore under the strain of the fierce wind.

"Quickly, we must get everyone down below deck," said Fujiwara. At that moment, a tall wave washed over the deck and carried his youngest son overboard. In desperation, Fujiwara jumped over the gunwale and tried to snatch the child from the clutching fingers of the violent waves. But he was too late.

"Stop the ships and release the lifeboats!" he cried to those on deck. All night long the sea raged as Fujiwara and his crew rowed the swells in search of the child. When morning broke, a calm settled over the wind and sea. As the sky cleared and the sun rose in the east, an exhausted crew lay sprawled on the decks. The child was lost.

Since there was nothing else they could do, the convoy continued on its journey. Fujiwara and his wife were grief-stricken over the loss of their beloved son. Husband and wife retired to their cabin and cried themselves to sleep.

A child dressed in a white frock appeared,
riding on the back of a great sea turtle.

As Fujiwara entered the land of dreams, a giant sea turtle appeared to him. "Yamakage," said the turtle, "have you lost faith? Do you not remember how you saved me from the cormorant fisherman who caught me in his net? Two years ago, in the Capital, you saw me captive and took pity upon me. You bought me from the fisherman, who was going to kill me for turtle soup. You saved my life. Now is my chance to show gratitude." With those words, the turtle pulled his head beneath the water and was gone.

"Sir, sir!" cried the captain as he shook Fujiwara from his slumber. "Come up on deck immediately. Something is swimming toward us and we do not know what it is."

Fujiwara and his wife jumped from their cot and soon stood looking over the railing where everyone was gathered. Closer and closer came a small, white object. "Perhaps it is a porpoise," said one of the hands.

"No, a porpoise would not ride upon the surface in that way," replied Fujiwara.

As it drew near, the figure of a child dressed in a white frock appeared. It was riding on the back of a great sea turtle. The smiling child looked perfectly content—splashing and playing with the water one moment, then holding tight onto the neck of the turtle whenever a wave broke over its shell.

Earth Tales from Around the World

"Look!" cried Fujiwara's wife. "Our son is coming back to us!"

She and her husband rowed out to meet their son. As they came to the turtle, they lifted the boy off its back and into the lifeboat. Through his tears, Fujiwara looked into the eyes of the great turtle and thanked him for his kindness.

At that joyous moment, Fujiwara finally remembered that two years ago, he had made a pilgrimage to the temple in Sumiyoshi. While he sailed toward the docks of that city, a cormorant fisherman pulled his boat alongside and offered his wares. Fujiwara saw a large turtle upon the fisherman's deck. As he gazed into the turtle's gentle eyes—the same eyes into which he was now staring—Fujiwara's heart had filled with compassion. He traded his own priceless pilgrimage cloak to the fisherman in exchange for the turtle. Then, he released the turtle back to his home in the sea.

Two years later, as the turtle's head once again disappeared beneath the waves, Fujiwara snapped out of his reverie. He realized that the great sea turtle had repaid his kindness by saving the life of his beloved son.

Turtle Returns the Gift

The Fairy Circle

Celtic
(Ireland and Scottish Highlands)

A FARMER AND HIS WIFE LIVED in the beautiful hill country of rolling fields, pastures and woodlands. The farmer worked hard, and he liked to see every bit of his land put to good use. On top of one hill, where the wind blew long through the fern and heather, was a circle of thorn trees where the *Daoine Sidhe,* the Fairy People, lived.

One day the farmer said to his wife, "That place on the hilltop has the best soil found on our land. I can't stand to see it wasted."

"You leave that place alone," she said sternly. "The Good People live there for sure. I often see them making merry as they travel down the hill, playing the fiddle, blowing the fife and singing their songs. Their laughter and dancing make the leaves quake with joy. They've never bothered us one bit, but if you go near their circle, they will be upon us in their anger."

"I think you're a bit daft," he replied. When his wife went back to her work, the farmer took his axe and walked up to the hilltop. He chopped down some of the thorn trees, pulled up the stumps with his oxen and planted a bit of seed in the freshly turned soil.

When the sun had set and the farmer was about to leave, he picked up a piece of branch from a thorn tree with which to feed the fire on the hearth at home. As he turned to leave, he heard voices behind. Looking back, he saw a strange glow coming from within the circle of trees. He strained in the dim light to see who was speaking but could find no one. Then he heard the blows of an axe.

"What are we going to do with the wood?" asked one voice.

"The farmer who lives nearby seems to be in dire need of wood," said another voice. "When we are done carving this tree, it will be in the image of his wife. We'll take his wife and leave this tree in her place. Just think of it, with a bit of magic he'll spend his days living with one of these trees, which he loves so dearly. He won't even know it is not his real wife." At that, the farmer heard peals of laughter as if the circle was filled with invisible people.

Down the hill he ran as fast as his legs would move. When he walked through the door, his wife saw that he was carrying a branch from a thorn tree.

The farmer heard peals of laughter as if the circle was filled with invisible people.

"What have you done?" she gasped.

"Nothing to get upset about," he said throwing the thorn log into the fire.

His wife rushed over to the hearth. "This tree belongs to the Good People," she said as she took it from the hearth and threw it out the door. "If we keep it, they will come after us to get it back."

"You've got nothing to worry about," said the farmer. Still, he was deathly afraid when he recalled the Fairies' scheme. He thought to himself, "No matter what I have to do, I will not let the Fairy People lay a hand on my wife." He bolted the doors and shuttered the windows before settling beneath the covers.

All night long, while his wife slept soundly, the farmer lay there with eyes wide. When the moon was high in the sky, a terrible cry split the silence. Out in the barn, the cows bellowed, the asses brayed and the pigs grunted as if beset by a terrible beast. The farmer could hear them straining against the locks and leads that held them.

"We should go check on the animals," said his wife. "Something is wrong out in the barn."

The Fairy Circle

"No! Stay inside. Neither of us will leave this place until the sun rises."

A strong gale shook the house and the animal cries grew louder.

"We have got to see if the animals need our help!" she cried rising from the bed.

"You'll do no such thing," said the farmer as he grabbed the back of her night clothes and pulled her down.

At that moment, the wind blew open the kitchen door and raced about the house. Cups, saucers and plates flew off the shelves and were smashed to pieces. Pots and pans clanged and crunched against one another, blowing about like leaves in a storm.

The farmer's wife kept trying to get up to check on the animals. "I'm not afraid," she said. But her husband held her hard by the arm and would not let go. Now there came strange voices and footsteps running up and down the halls and into the doorway of the bedroom.

"Who is there?" screamed the woman. "What do you want? Leave us be!" For the rest of the night the strangers rampaged and plundered. They tugged on the arms of the farmer's wife, but he held her fast around the waist and would not let go.

When the sun finally broke over the hilltops, the wind and the raging quieted. The farmer and his wife arose and walked out to the kitchen. In the midst of the rubble lay a wooden carving in the exact likeness of the woman. In their frustration at not being able to carry her off, the Fairies had flown about the house and left the image behind.

"Who did this and why?" asked the farmer's wife. At last, the farmer told her the entire story about what he overheard the night before as he listened from the edge of the Fairy Circle.

"You fool!" she said. "Didn't I warn you?"

Such is the wrath of the Fairies when their trees are cut down, and the circles in which they dwell are disturbed.

Some folk say that the Fairies are fallen angels who watch over the trees, flowers, animals and all of Earth. They take offense at being called anything but the Good People. When human beings do good deeds, the Good People repay them in kind. But when human beings act unkindly toward the natural world, or toward each other, the Good People repay them with unkindness. Because Fairies can take the form of flowers, butterflies and other small beings in nature, we must treat them all especially well. One can never tell when a blossom or an insect is really a Fairy in disguise.

150

The Pumpkin Seed Bird

Creole
(MARTINIQUE)

ONCE THERE WAS A KIND OLD WOMAN who lived in a straw hut and slept on a cushion of dried grass. Although she was lonely and had suffered much in her many years, she always had a kind word for others. Because she was too weak to catch the crawfish, *zabitan,* who lived in the rushing waters of the river, the old woman ate mostly watercress.

One morning, as she was out gathering sticks for firewood, she saw something thrashing about in the tall grass. She walked closer, parted the leaves and saw a wounded bird. "I must take this bird home and make it well again," she thought.

The old woman gently picked up the wounded bird and held it close to her breast. Back home, she cleaned the wound and poured in a bit of camphor to keep it from becoming infected. As the days passed, and the old woman continued to eat her watercress, she fed the bird seeds, berries and sugar water. Often, she petted its beautiful feathers. Each night she wrapped the bird in her cotton bedding and sang lullabies to give it comfort. In time, she tenderly nursed the bird back to health.

When the bird was well enough to live on its own, the old woman carried it to the same place where she had found it. She held the bird up against her wrinkled cheek, stroked it a few times and said good-bye. Then she carefully placed the bird on the ground. The bird flapped and stretched its wings, looked up at its friend and flew away. The old woman walked slowly back to her hut. When she entered and saw the many things that reminded her of the bird, she felt more lonely than ever.

Many days passed. One morning, the old woman went out to gather watercress. On the way, a wingtip brushed against her cheek. There, perched on the limb of a tree, was the little bird. It flew down, dropped a pumpkin seed at the old woman's feet, and winged away as it filled the air with song.

The thought of eating pumpkin pleased the old woman beyond words. She went straight home and planted the little seed. With the watering and weeding, the loving care she gave the young plant, it grew quickly and flowered. In a short time it formed many round pumpkins. When at last the old woman picked the first ripe pumpkin, it was a perfect shape and size. She brought it into the hut, placed it upon the table and cut it open. Inside, to her surprise

151

The little bird flew down and dropped a pumpkin seed
at the old woman's feet.

and delight, she found a delicious cooked meal of meat and rice, well spiced and ready to be eaten. Her hungry heart leaped at the sight. The first few bites reminded her of all the wonderful tastes and smells of her own mother's cooking. Her stomach was so shrunken from eating watercress that the third bite satisfied her completely.

Being far too much for the old woman to eat, she took the rest of the meal and shared it with her neighbor, who owned nothing but a pepper plant.

"Oh, *Oh!*" cried the old woman's neighbor, "this is the most delicious meal I can ever remember eating. Where did you get it?"

"Come to my hut at midday tomorrow, and I will show you," said the old woman. "We will share another meal."

At noon the next day, and every day that followed, a new pumpkin ripened on the vine. Every ripe pumpkin that the old woman opened contained another tasty meal. Each meal was something different and delicious to eat.

Even though the old woman always shared her meals, her neighbor envied the pumpkin vine. Often, while they were eating a hearty meal, the old woman shared her story of how she came to have the pumpkin seed that she had planted.

Secretly, her neighbor thought, "I want to have a pumpkin vine like that of my own." For many days she went out and searched the brush for a wounded bird to save. But she found none. Finally, in desperation, she picked up a stone and threw it at the next bird she saw. When she picked up the wounded bird, it looked exactly like the bird the old woman had described as the one she had nursed back to life.

The selfish neighbor took the bird home, washed the wound and tossed the bird down on the floor. When she awoke the next day, she carried the bird outside and heaved it up into the air. Because there was a strong wind blowing, the wounded bird was able to flap its feeble wings just enough to drift up over the trees away from that woman's hut. The woman kept an impatient, watchful eye on the sky.

A few days later, the little bird flew over and threw a pumpkin seed at the neighbor. She planted and watered the seed, which grew, flowered and bore many plump, beautiful pumpkins. When the first pumpkin ripened, the woman exclaimed, "Now I will have a feast of my own!"

When she cut the pumpkin in half, a stinking, writhing ball of lizards, snakes and spiders crawled out and tried to bite her. She ran away so fast, they say, that she rose up into the wind and blew off to a distant land, never to return.

The Pumpkin Seed Bird

Lessons

See the "Activities" section for ideas on how to explore these lessons.

Disappearing Flowers is an Arab story from Syria in which a prince finds true love when he risks his life to save his parents' rarest flower. The scent of the rarest flower fills people's hearts with hope, but a gigantic, hideous beast is stealing the blossoms. The story contains a clear lesson for today: When we do not take care of the threatened and endangered species in our world we are like the thieving monster in this story—we rob the world of hope for the future. We steal from the children yet to come, whose lives would have been enriched by the survival of those species. At the end of this story, the prince and the princess set an example of wise stewardship by taking care of the rarest flowers.

This Japanese story, **Turtle Returns the Gift,** is about keeping strong the Circle of Giving and Receiving between people and animals. A Japanese statesman, Fujiwara saves a sea turtle from being killed by a fisherman, then releases the turtle in the sea. Two years later, when Fujiwara's son is lost at sea in a terrible storm, the same turtle saves the boy's life and returns him safely to his parents. We all travel in the Circle of Life. Whatever we bring into the Circle with how we live our lives, comes back around to us.

In **The Fairy Circle,** a farmer's wife tells him to leave the circle of thorn trees alone because the fairies live there. This story warns us to be careful when and how we cut trees or disturb the plants that live in the forest. The Celtic people believe in a strong connection between fairies and the natural world. This farmer, who cannot leave even one patch of his land untilled, learns that bad things can happen when we do not act kindly toward plants. The fairies make sure we remember this lesson and that we treat nature with respect.

The Pumpkin Seed Bird is a Creole story about showing care and compassion for the little things in nature and being satisfied with what we have. A poor, pure-hearted old woman saves a wounded bird and is rewarded for her kindness. The bird gives her a pumpkin seed that grows pumpkins filled with delicious meals. Because we know so little about the value of things living in nature, we do a great deed every time we save even a small part of the natural world. The old woman's greedy, envious neighbor, however, schemes to get the bird to bring her a pumpkin seed, too. She harms the bird and pretends to save it. This woman's reward, in kind, is a pumpkin full of snakes, lizards and spiders. In our relationship with the natural world, we reap what we sow.

154

Ten

Wisdom

The Wisdom of Nature

Swahili
(KENYA, TANZANIA AND ZANZIBAR)

IN THE THICK BRUSH AT THE EDGE OF THE HILL COUNTRY lived a magnificent snake. Its eyes blazed and the scales that covered its skin were as hard and strong as any shield. Venom flowed from its long, curved fangs. In the moment of its hunger, this huge, powerful snake devoured any wild animal it desired.

One day, the snake sat sunning itself in a small clearing. Being close to the ground, the snake sensed a roar in the distance. Its tongue picked up a strong scent. Upwind, some young hunters were burning the brush to drive the game animals into the open. Crackling flames rushed toward the snake.

As it searched for refuge, the snake slithered out of the low brush and into the open along the border of a farmer's fields.

"Please help me hide," asked the snake. "The hunters are coming. They will kill me."

When he saw the snake, the farmer was afraid.

"Do not fear me," the snake called out to the farmer. "I will not harm you."

The kindhearted farmer took pity on the snake, as he did on all animals that were in need of help.

"Quickly," said the farmer as he opened the mouth of a large, empty grain bag, "crawl into this sack. The hunters will never think to look for you here."

As soon as the tip of the snake's tail disappeared into the mouth of the bag, some hunters approached. They were following the faint trail left by the snake's belly as it slid along the ground.

"Have you seen a large snake come this way?" they asked the farmer.

"No," he replied. "I have been working here all morning and have seen no sign of a snake. You must be reading an old trail."

"Thank you," said the hunters, and they walked on. When they were a safe distance away, the farmer opened the grain bag and whispered, "Come out, the danger has passed."

The snake crept out of the sack, threw its coils around the farmer and held him fast.

"Let me go!" screamed the farmer. "I have just saved your life!"

"That is true," replied the snake. "But I have not eaten for many days. You will make a good meal."

157

"Let me go!" screamed the farmer. "I have just saved your life!"

"Then you will not let me go?" asked the farmer.

"No, I am starving."

"Before you eat me," said the farmer, "you could at least repay me for saving your life."

"That is only fair," said the snake. "I agree. Now what do you desire?"

"Let us have others decide whether you should eat me."

"If that is your wish, so be it," agreed the snake.

The snake followed the farmer to the edge of the field where a coconut palm tree had been planted. The tree listened carefully as each of them told his side of the story.

"Well," replied the coconut palm, "I know the nature of human beings. They eat my nuts and drink the sweet milk inside. Some even use my leaves to thatch their roofs. Why should I save a human being? I say the snake should have its meal."

"Let us ask the bee," said the farmer.

"As you wish," replied the snake.

"You must be joking!" replied the bee. "Human beings smoke us out of our homes and steal our honey. They never give us thanks. I have no compassion for the farmer."

"Perhaps the mango tree down by the road will understand my plight," thought the farmer. "Snake, let us go ask the mango to give us its judgment."

"Lead on," replied the snake.

Once it had listened to their stories, the mango tree spoke. "Year after year I stand here as generations of human beings pass by. They cool themselves in the shade of my branches and eat my fruit when they are hungry. Some break off my branches for firewood or to use as the shafts of spears for hunting the wild animals. Not once has a human being thanked me. Farmer, I see no reason why the snake should not eat you."

"How could this be?" exclaimed the farmer. "Why should my life be such a trifle in the eyes of Nature?"

At that moment, the farmer spotted a gazelle grazing along the riverbank. To the gazelle the farmer now pleaded his case.

In response to his story, the gazelle told a tale of its own. "I am often the difference between life and death for the human beings. Without my meat, they would starve and perish. Because I am so generous, people take me for granted. Your life, farmer, belongs to the snake."

159

A baboon was listening from where it sat on the branch of a nearby tree.

"Every creature does what it must in order to survive," said the baboon. "That is the way of Nature."

"But what of the snake?" asked the farmer.

The Wisdom of Nature

"One cannot blame the snake for its hunger," replied the baboon. "Like you, the snake is part of the balance that exists in the world."

A snake is meant to eat its prey,
it catches as it can.
Its food will try to get away,
escape's the way of man.

"What, then, do you have to say about whether or not I should eat the farmer?" asked the snake.

"First, you must show me exactly how it happened," said the baboon. "That sack does not look big enough to hold a snake as magnificent as yourself."

The farmer then opened the bag and the snake crawled in.

"Are you able to close the bag with the snake inside?" asked the baboon.

"Yes," replied the farmer as he drew the cord tight and tied it securely.

"Now, farmer, we will see what you have learned," said the baboon. "Once again, the fate of the snake is in your hands."

160

Four Who Made a Tiger

Kannada
(INDIA)

A WEALTHY COUPLE FROM THE CITY OF FLOWERS had four sons. Because the boys were raised by Brahmin parents, they were members of the highest Hindu caste in society. Soon after the brothers had grown into manhood, their mother and father died. Before they realized what was happening, relatives had stolen all of their inheritance.

"There is nothing left for us in this village," said one brother. "Perhaps we should visit our mother's father."

"But it is several days' journey," said another. "We have no food or money."

"We will simply have to beg and make do with what little we have along the way," said the third brother.

In a few days, the four brothers arrived at their grandfather's house, only to find that he had died months ago. Still, their cousins took them in and gave them something to eat. During the next few weeks, the cousins provided food, shelter and work, but they treated the four brothers poorly and ridiculed them.

Finally, the brothers could stand it no longer. "Brothers," said the eldest, "we must leave this place and go off to make our way. We are young and have our wits to rely upon. That is all we really need. Poverty is a temporary thing like the morning fog. Soon, the clouds will disappear and the sun will shine down upon us."

"What shall we do for a living?" asked the youngest brother.

"If we begin the journey, the answer will come to us," replied the eldest. "Each of us must go out into the world and learn a skill. Once we have done that, we will come back together and learn from one another. When all of our learning is put together, we will have great power."

Several years passed before the brothers assembled at the agreed upon time and place.

"Let us see what we have learned," said one of the brothers as they wandered around. In time, they found a tiger's thighbone lying alongside the trail.

The first brother picked up the thighbone, studied it and said, "I have learned how to take a bone such as this and create the entire skeleton of an animal." As soon as he had finished speaking, the tiger's skeleton was made whole.

"Hmm," said the second brother. "The skill that I have learned is how to restore the flesh and muscle to the bones of an animal. This I can do." With

161

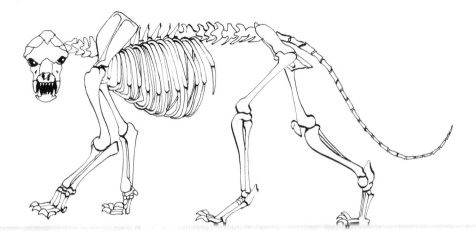

As soon as the first brother was finished speaking,
the tiger's skeleton was made whole.

those words, he stooped over the tiger's skeleton and began to work in earnest. When he stepped back, the tiger's flesh and muscle were restored.

"Now it is clear that our journey of learning had a purpose," said the third brother. "A sage whom I met along the way taught me how to cover an animal with skin and fur." In a short time, the animal took on the appearance of a finished tiger.

"Well, I can see that we all need each other," said the fourth brother. "What good would this tiger be without me? I can bring such an animal to life." Then he began to recite incantations and work his magic. Slowly, the tiger's chest began to heave as it took its first breath. The great eyes opened and in them the brothers could see a deep hunger. The tiger flexed its paws and claws. Then it rolled over onto its feet and stood in a daze. When it saw the four men standing around it, the tiger let out a tremendous roar and pounced on the brothers. In a tangle of biting teeth and slashing claws, the tiger killed and ate the four men. As the beast walked away in search of a place to rest, it left behind nothing but the bones of the four brothers.

The brothers had mastered their skills well. But such skills will only bring about goodness when they are used with intelligence and wisdom.

162

The Silkies &
the Fisherman's Sons

Gypsy/Traveller
(SCOTLAND)

ON THE WEST COAST OF SCOTLAND, there once lived a hardy *crofter*, a farmer, and his family. Their sturdy, stone-walled house rose from the rainy, windswept fields carpeted with heath and heather. This crofter's land swept up from the coast and reached to the next ridge of hills. When the crofter walked in these quiet, open spaces, his spirit soared with the breeze that blew in from the sea to brush the mountaintops. His family had a few horses, some cattle and many sheep that grazed the hillsides.

The farmer and his wife also had five sons. They had added to their wee house with each new member of the family, until it had become a large, comfortable home. Still, the family had outgrown the lands of the crofter, and his sons needed to find work elsewhere in order to survive.

When he was young, the crofter had been a fisherman. He had taken up crofting, in addition to fishing, in order to support his growing family. But now he was weary of fishing and getting too old to sail out upon the sea.

"Father," said one of his sons, "we'll have to leave the croft if we can't find more work. One day we'll have families of our own. Then what will we do?"

"I've been thinking about this very thing," said their father. "I don't want you to have to leave. Besides, if you did go, I couldn't possibly do all of the work around the croft by myself."

"Well, Father, what can we do?"

"You three young boys take the boat and the nets and do the best you can to make a living from the sea. Your two older brothers and I will have just enough work between us here at the croft."

The crofter spent many days out in the bay beyond the croft, showing the young boys how to set and haul the nets. Fishing was good there, but it was much better near the large island that lay a few miles offshore. There they could sail and fill their nets to near bursting with fish.

On some days, though, when they hauled their nets, many of the cod and other fish had been eaten. The island was home to hundreds of seals.

"Look, Father," said his sons, "the seals have been at our fish again!"

"Yes, I see," said the crofter. "The seal folk have indeed been at the fish. But don't you forget lads, they have families, too, who need to eat just like we do."

For many months the fisherman's sons worked hard and had good catches. They took the fish to a nearby town and sold them in the fish market. As the season wore on, however, the seals ate more and more of the fish. Sometimes they chewed holes in the nets, sometimes the fish were missing fins or tails.

"I'm proud of you boys," their father said one night when they returned home. "You've learned well and worked hard."

"But Father," complained one of his young sons, "it's harder and harder to make enough money to live on. The seals eat many of our fish and chew others up so badly that we cannot sell them."

"Now sons, I lived with the seals my whole life. While you were growing up, I was able to raise you by fishing and working the croft. Sometimes I had to share the fish with the seals. It seems only fair—those seal folk have hungry children of their own. They are good people who only take what they need."

"Father, that may be true, but one day we are going to have families, too. If we have just enough fish to support ourselves now, what are we going to do when we have wives and children?"

"Enough of that!" yelled their father. "I'm tired of hearing about the seals. Those people have been kind to me, and I to them. If you don't stop this complaining, only bad can come of it."

From that day on, although the seals continued to eat the fish and damage their nets, the young men never said another word to their father about it.

On some evenings, as the boys sailed to Seal Island, they sang this song:

> *Now we fill our sails,*
> *to the Isle of Seals we go.*
> *There we'll set our nets adrift*
> *and haul our catch in tow.*

On every side of the island, steep cliffs faced the sea. There was only one quiet cove where the land dipped down to meet the waves, where driftwood collected and the strong odor of rotting seaweed filled the air. There, at sunset, the young fishermen often saw hundreds of seals hauling out onto the rocks to bask. On one such evening, the oldest of the three boys had an idea.

"This is what we are going to do," he explained to his brothers. "Tomorrow night, when the seals climb up onto the rocks, we are going to be waiting for them. With clubs and stones we will kill the young seals and drive the older ones away. Then we will have the fish all to ourselves."

The next day came and went. As their mother cleaned up after dinner, and their father and older brothers were occupied with the evening chores, the three younger boys stole quietly down to the shore. They loaded their clubs into the boat and rowed off to Seal Island. The red rays of sunlight reflected off the calm waters, as their song echoed through the damp stillness.

O'er the sunset waters,
to the Isle of Seals we row.
There we'll wait the evening hours
and catch them in the cove.

As the young fishermen neared the island, they hauled in the oars and drifted toward the cove.

"I have a strange feeling," said one of the sons. "There's not a seal in sight. Where could they be?"

"Don't you worry," said the oldest among them. "They'll be here soon enough. They always come."

The young men hid their boat at the mouth of the cove. They climbed the rocks and waited quietly for the seals. About an hour passed in the cold evening breeze. A storm was coming and drizzle began to soak through the boys' clothing. The youngest boy shivered. "We had better build a wee fire to keep warm," he said. They made a small pile of driftwood and set it ablaze.

"What's that?" asked one of the boys. "I hear voices coming toward us."

"No, that's just the wind," said another.

Then dark shapes moved like liquid up the rocks. Soon a few hundred of them stood before the boys. The biggest and oldest were in front, with the young ones behind. The firelight flickered on the faces of the strange creatures, who looked like people but were half-covered with thick coats of fur dripping with seawater. They were *Silkies:* seal folk who had taken the form of men, women and children of all sizes.

Now the boys were more horrified than they had ever been. The trail to the cove was blocked. The only other way off the island was over the steep cliffs!

The largest, roughest-looking Silkie began to speak in mixed Gaelic and English. Between the words came snorts, growls and grunts. It was a strange, broken language of land and sea. The boys understood the Gaelic language and could just make out the meaning of the words.

"Here they are! Let's get them! We know what you came here for. You came to kill us and our wee children!"

"But we never meant any harm to you and your folk," said the oldest brother. "We do not even know you. Where are you from and why do you think we mean to bring harm to you?"

"Don't you know who we are? Take a good look."

The boys strained their eyes in the dim, dancing light. They gasped.

165

"That's right, I can see it in your eyes now," said the Silkie. "We are the very seal folk you sailed out here to kill tonight. And now, we are going to do to you as you would have done to us. Prepare to die!"

A mob surrounded the young men, who held on to each other, shaking with fear. The Silkies picked up stones and driftwood and raised them over their heads.

The Silkies & the Fisherman's Sons

The most ancient of the Silkies came toward the boys.

Suddenly, the crowd parted and the most ancient of the Silkies came toward the boys, leaning on a driftwood cane. He was stooped over from the years. His stiff beard looked like layers of wizened seaweed that waved in the sea breeze. "Halt!" he cried out. "Do not cast a single stone!"

"But Grandfather," said the big, strong one who had been the first to speak. "They came here to do us harm!"

"'Tis true," replied the old one. Then he turned to face the three sons.

"We know what ye came here for. How many times did yer father tell ye to let the seal folk be? The waters around this island, and the fish ye catch in them, belong to us. We take the fish that we need to feed ourselves and our young ones. Ye boys are lucky," said the old one, "even though ye don't deserve it."

Then he wheeled around to face the mob. "Let them go," he yelled. "Do not harm a hair on their heads!"

Low, guttural voices swept through the crowd like a breaking wave. "But Grandfather, why should we let them go? They came here to kill us!"

"Aye, that's true," he replied. "But if it weren't for the father of these boys, I would have died when I was young. Ye would never have been born. One day, their father was out fishing, and I swam into his net after some fish. I got wrapped up and struggled until I nearly drowned. At that moment, their father hauled me up, untangled me and kindly released me. Now, we are going to let these young men go."

"But listen well," he said to the boys. "The fish in these here waters belong to us. Ye can fish elsewhere. From this day forth, whatever ye do to the seal folk, we are going to do to ye. Treat us well and we will do the same to ye."

At this, the crowd parted and the young men, seeing their path to freedom, ran and slipped over the dark, uneven rocks toward the shore. They jumped into the boat and rowed their hearts out without ever looking back.

At last, they docked the boat and walked through the door of their house.

"Well, boys," asked their father, "where have you been? You look kind of weary and pale."

"We didn't go anywhere really, father," said one of his sons. "We just rowed out to Seal Island to see how the fish were running."

"Now boys, what did I tell you?"

"We know, father. And we've been thinking that maybe you're right. We're not going to set our nets in the waters around the island any more. Those fish belong to the seal folk, just like you've always said."

That was the last time the three young fishermen ever journeyed to Seal Island.

167

The Garden of Wisdom

Jewish
(ISRAEL)

A KING ONCE SAID THAT PEOPLE should not be given their position in life by birth or wealth. "It is my belief," he told his three sons, "that people should earn their standing in life according to who they have become and what they have accomplished by their own deeds. It does not matter to me into what family or kingdom a person is born, unless he has done something of value and nobility."

When the king's three sons were full grown, he took them into his chamber and spoke. "As you know, you have, by birthright, been given much wealth and privilege. I love you all very much and my heart desires to keep you close. And there is much work to be done here in the kingdom. But, it is time for you to go into the world and show me who you are and what you are capable of doing. Thus, I am sending you on a long journey. This is your chance to accomplish something of greatness and to prove that you are worthy of serving in a position of authority and responsibility. When the time comes, I will send a ship to bring you home."

"Father, we are ready and anxious for this journey to begin," said the princes.

In two days, the three princes found themselves sailing toward the land of the Moors. On the way, they spotted a lush, green island on which there was a beautiful, walled garden. The great ship slipped into the harbor and the princes rowed to shore. In front of the garden gate stood three guardians. As the princes approached, they were greeted by a guard who was ancient and stooped.

"You are welcome to enter this garden, in which you will find many pleasures. You may stay for some time but, one day, you will have to leave."

Then, a second guardian spoke to the young men. She was very sick, with bumps and sores on her skin. "The fruits and delights in this garden are a feast for those who enter. But you can take nothing with you when you leave."

When the princes looked at the third guardian, they saw that he was a clean, handsome man of about the same age as their father.

"Be careful and keep safe your souls," said this guardian. "Eat only the sound, ripe fruit. Do not pick or eat any fruit that is not yet ready, or which has gone by and begun to spoil."

Each tree was heavy with delicious, ripe fruit.
Gems and pearls glistened from the ground.

As they stepped through the garden gate, their eyes sparkled. Each tree was heavy with delicious, ripe fruit. Gems and pearls glistened from the ground, which was also laced with streams and rivers like fingers of clean, pure water embracing the fertile, green earth. When the princes tasted the water, they found that it was a sweet nectar. Each prince began to wander around the garden on his own.

One of the brothers could not keep his eyes off of the colorful rubies, diamonds, sapphires and countless other gems strewn upon the ground. He began to fill his pockets and thought of how he could carry away enough

The Garden of Wisdom

wealth to last a lifetime. When his pockets were full, he removed his shirt, tied off the cuffs to make a sac and filled it with riches. Next, he took off and filled his pants, then his briefs, socks and cap. Soon, this prince was walking around naked, straining to carry his clothes laden with riches. The prince was so afraid that something might happen to his wealth that he hefted its great weight everywhere he went. He was so consumed with gathering and guarding his gems that he did not eat. In time, he grew pale, weak and sickly.

The second prince wandered in search of the perfect piece of fruit, the sweetest spring from which to quench his thirst. He became so completely lost in pursuit of satisfying his tongue that he did not notice how obese he was growing.

"Look at this!" said the third prince to his brothers. "See how many different kinds of trees and flowers grow in this garden. This plant smells like it could have healing properties. Here is a kind of mineral that I have never seen before! Who could have created such a perfect world of nature on this island?" But the two other princes were so absorbed in pursuing their pleasures that they did not hear their brother.

In time, the third prince saw how everything in the garden had its place and that the workings of all the living things moved to the same rhythm in a dance of life. The streams and rivers were full during the months when the plants most needed the water to grow their flowers, fruit and seeds. As he wandered and wondered at his surroundings, he ate and drank only what he needed to retain health and vigor, savoring every mouthful. "There must be some great, wise and unseen force that created this perfect world," he thought. "It could not possibly have arisen by chance. If only I could meet someone who could answer my questions."

One day, after several seasons had passed, a ship sailed into the harbor. The three brothers were called to the garden gate. A Moor, a messenger from their father, told the princes that the king had summoned them. "My sons, it is time for you to return home. You are to leave with haste and return to the palace. Your ship awaits."

As the three princes left the garden, the guardians beat and mocked the one who labored under the weight of his jewels and gems. "See how you have wasted away to nothing," they said. "And it was all for nought because you cannot bring any of your treasure beyond these gates." At that, they wrestled all of the prince's wealth from him and scattered it once again over the garden grounds.

"Look at yourself," said the guardians to the second prince as he approached the gates. "You have eaten so many pieces of plump fruit that you are now shaped like one. Your tongue has defeated you."

When the third prince emerged from the garden, the guardians said respectfully, "Good sir, allow us to escort you to the ship."

170

As the three brothers rowed out to the ship that was waiting in the harbor, the one who had been eating and drinking for many months, and who was enormously obese, collapsed and died of exertion. Caught suddenly in their grief during the long journey home, the other two princes held a memorial service and buried their brother at sea.

When, at last, the two brothers reached the palace gates, the guards did not recognize the one who had wasted away. In his sadness over losing his brother and his fortune and at being humiliated by the guardians of the garden, this prince continued to neglect his body. When the guards refused to allow him to enter the palace, he began to cry and beg for them to allow him to pass. Even though the king sent a letter to the guards saying that this was his son, they drove him from the kingdom.

When the guards turned toward the third prince, they cried, "Welcome, your highness." This son was led with great dignity and celebration through the grounds of the palace and into the king's chamber.

The king rose and embraced the prince warmly as tears welled up in his eyes and flowed down into his thick, gray beard. "I am glad to have you home again, son. But I am also heartsick over the fate of your brothers."

"Father, I am glad to be home, yet I will miss my brothers dearly. It has been a difficult journey getting back."

"But you should have seen the island and the garden where we spent these many months. It is a beautiful place where the birds, animals and plants live in complete harmony. Many things live there that we do not have in our kingdom. I have wandered for months and have tried to understand how all of these things live together so completely, and who could possibly have created such a wondrous place."

Again the king held his son close and kissed him. "Sit, and I will answer all of your questions." For many hours they met in quiet counsel as the king satisfied the prince's burning curiosity.

Finally, the king said to his son, "I am glad to see that you did not spend your time seeking earthly pleasures in the garden. Many people are only interested in gathering wealth during the course of their lives. In the end, these poor, empty lives have been wasted. Others are consumed with satisfying the pleasures of the body. Their lives are brief. You have chosen to find delight and meaning in understanding Creation and the mystery that lies beyond this world. Your reward will be great."

171

Lessons

See the "Activities" section for ideas on how to explore these lessons.

This story from the Swahili people, **The Wisdom of Nature,** tells us that every creature has its own way of surviving in the natural world. Just as the snake must prey upon the animals and the people, the caring farmer cannot ignore the snake's plea for help. The coconut palm, the bee, the mango tree and the gazelle, however, are not pleased with how they have given so much to human beings and have never been thanked or treated well in return. The baboon then speaks of how the world is in balance when everything lives by its true nature. In the end, the farmer is again given the chance to decide the fate of the snake based on what he has learned from nature.

Four Who Made a Tiger is a powerful story from the Kannada people of India. It shows how the four brothers learned important skills that were even more potent when used together. Like scientists who have figured out how an animal is made, the brothers combine their knowledge and create a living tiger from a single bone. Because the brothers do not think about the consequences of their actions, they pay the ultimate price. This story cautions us to be humble in what we do with our skills and wisdom and to take care not to play the role of the Creator. These are lessons we would do well to keep in mind today, as the sciences of biological and genetic engineering give us new ways to shape our world.

In the Gypsy story, **The Silkies & the Fisherman's Sons,** the three youngest sons of a man who is a crofter and fisherman, learn to strike a balance between meeting their own needs and allowing the seals to meet theirs. They learn that wild animals, too, have families and a right to feed them—wisdom their father was sharing all along. Because of youth and inexperience, the fisherman's sons almost lose their lives, but they are spared when an ancient Silkie remembers that the boys' father saved his life years ago. The wisdom of the elders shows the boys that whatever we do to the natural world, we do to ourselves. This story also shows how overhunting endangers the seals' survival.

The Garden of Wisdom shows how we determine who we are by the choices we make in our lives. Virtue comes from acting wisely. One of the three princes falls prey to greed and another is lured into a deadly trap of gluttony. The third prince spends his time seeking to understand the mysteries of the Creator, the rhythms of life and the harmony he sees in the ways of the natural world. This Jewish tale reminds us that wealth and physical pleasures do not last long, but wisdom and virtue are everlasting.

172

First Tail, Last Tale

Tell Tails

Maya
(Guatemala and Mexico)

WHEN THE WORLD WAS NEW, only dogs could speak about Creation. They traveled widely and shared many of the Creator's secrets.

"This will not do," the Creator told the dogs. "You must stop revealing my secrets." But the dogs continued to speak freely about the mysteries of Creation.

"Very well," said the Creator, "this is how it is going to be. From now on your busy tongues will be placed behind you, and what I first put in the rear will then move to your head."

As soon as he said these words, the dogs' wagging tongues appeared behind them. Because they could not speak, dogs were no longer able to share the secrets of Creation. From that day forward, whenever a dog tries to express itself, the tongue-that-became-a-tail wags instead.

175

Whenever a dog tries to express itself,
the tongue-that-became-a-tail wags instead.

Activities

Choose the lessons you want to explore from among those provided at the end of each of the ten sections of stories. Bring those lessons to life using one or more of the activities from the following list. There are no "right" or "wrong" responses to many of these questions/activities. They are designed to help you explore the world around you, your place in the natural order and the lives of other peoples.

ACTIVITIES ABOUT THE EARTH

- Grow a sense of place. Go into a natural area and spend some time alone and in silence. Adopt and do something good for that area. Give a gift to the plants or animals who live there to show that you care for and appreciate them. Visit often.
- Create a model of some part of Earth, or some living things, in order to better understand them. Do this after you read stories that explore the stars, volcanoes, animals, plants and so on. Models can take any form, such as dioramas, clay sculptures or creations made of other materials.
- Identify and study current environmental issues relating to those in the stories. Prepare "news reports" about these issues, including written articles, photographs and/or video reports.
- Design some team projects through which you can became involved in environmental activities suggested by a story's setting or lessons.
- Take a field trip to visit a natural habitat or other setting in which you can explore a lesson from a story.
- Create an inventory of the plants and animals around your home, learning center or library environment. Become acquainted with the real-life characters with which you share your home space. Do something to benefit the natural world around you. (See the following activity for some suggestions.)
- Refer to the list of the plants and animals that live in your area described in the previous activity. Think of all of the wonderful things they bring into your lives. For example, flowers give us beauty, nectar for honey, seeds and fruits. Now think of ways of completing the Circle and giving something back. In the case of flowers, this may take the form of planting more flowers, preserving them, creating a wildflower garden or drawing pictures of them to show your appreciation.
- Identify the serious environmental/ethical issues raised by a story, such as those from the story from India, **Four Who Made a Tiger.** Create a role-playing exercise through which you will study and defend different sides of the issue by becoming real-life, contemporary figures, such as government officials, representatives from conservation groups, members of the general public, people from Native cultures and so on. Be sure to set some ground rules and appoint a moderator to maintain order during the discussion/debate. After everyone has had their say about the issue, have the group try to decide what is the best course of action to take.
- Follow today's news reports about the cultures and environments from which these stories come.
- Begin long-term activities, such as vegetable gardens, litter patrols, butterfly gardens and other ongoing community projects, which will be carried on for several seasons or years. Hand these projects down to younger children.

- Keep journals to record your experiences, thoughts and feelings related to the stories and activities you take part in. Include whatever you desire, such as prose, poetry, illustrations, photographs, music and so on.
- Work as a group to create maps of where natural habitats similar to those that occur in a story are found near your home or learning center, such as wetlands, forests and fields. Visit these areas to conduct some of the environmental activities described in this section.
- List the plants, animals and natural habitats mentioned in a particular story. Visit similar habitats in your area and look for close relatives of those plants and animals from local environments. (See the following activity.)
- Use the list you made in the previous activity and create riddles that describe particular plants, animals or people from that story. Share these riddles with others. Can they solve them?
- Draw a picture of the most beautiful place you can imagine. Ask yourself, "What is it that makes a place beautiful?" Where would you live if you could choose any place?
- Develop environmental story lessons into cooperative, group-building conservation projects such as recycling, conserving energy, preserving land, protecting endangered species, picking up litter and planting trees.
- Design and become active in community conservation activities.
- Go on an outing during which you share stories and outdoor activities such as a hike, an evening campfire, a camping trip or a bicycle ride.
- Dress up as a plant or animal from a story and hold a party that everyone attends in costume.
- Go on a scavenger hunt and try to find things that are similar to those that are part of a story, such as leaves, nuts, flowers, animals (in the wild or in a zoo), images in an art museum and architectural designs. Purchase a plant that is native to that part of the world the story comes from and grow it in the home or learning center.
- Create a game in which you match the plants or animals from a particular story with their survival adaptations (claws, thorns, seed parachutes, etc.).
- Find in your community some natural or human-made materials or structures that relate to a story. Create rubbings of these items using large pieces of newsprint and crayons or pastels.
- Study the natural habitats of the cultures from which these stories come. Explore ways in which a culture's environment can affect how people live and how their culture develops.
- Find pictures and artwork in magazines that come from the culture and environment presented by a particular story. Search in magazines such as *National Geographic, Natural History, International Wildlife* and *Audubon.* Use these images to create a scrapbook, or glue them onto cardboard and cut them into puzzles.
- After you read a story, choose something or someone you liked, such as a person, plant or animal. Draw or describe in words that person or thing. Share the illustration or description with others and see if they can guess which person or thing you have chosen and described.
- Share stories about the forces of Nature, such as weather, volcanoes, seasonal changes and so on. Now set up a monitoring program and keep track of these forces on the local, national and global level. Study what is behind these forces, such as those that drive the weather or form volcanoes and cause them to erupt. Keep track of these events and patterns using journals, charts, maps, press clippings, weekly reports etc.
- Share your Earth projects with other groups and ask them to share theirs.

ACTIVITIES ABOUT STORIES AND CULTURES

- Turn a story into a puppet show or play to perform. A performance can take the shape of a play in which everyone has their own lines and performs in character. Another, simpler kind of play is one in which a narrator reads the play while characters act out their parts silently. If you choose to put on a performance, have everyone make a costume to appear as they imagine their plant or animal appears in the story. Consult encyclopedias to get information about the appearance of plants and animals from around the world. Because many cultures consider it to be disrespectful for others to try to imitate their traditional dress, it is better to avoid doing this. (See the following activity.)

- Share a story together and find materials that explore the sensory experiences as everyone imagines them in the story. Re-create some of the sounds, smells, sights, tastes and senses of touch that you can identify in the story. Incorporate these into the performance described in the previous activity.

- Create a fantasy. Change the names in the stories to those of people in your group. Have someone read the story while everyone else sits silently, with eyes closed, and imagines they are characters in the story.

- Draw a picture of what you think a particular scene from a story looks like.

- Change something in one of these stories to make it out of character with the rest of the story. Read the story to others and see if they can discover the change.

- Read a story from this book. Now, create two stories—one that tells what you think happened before the original story, and one that describes what takes place after the original story. Create different kinds of stories from the voice of the first person (I, we), second person (you) and third person (they, them) perspectives.

- Discuss or write about the way you felt as you read or listened to the story. Why did you feel that way? Which characters did you identify with the most?

- Whom do you like, and dislike, from a story? Why do you feel the way you do? What makes a person likable or disagreeable?

- Post a large copy of a map of the world on a bulletin board. Stick a pin in the map marking the location of each story as you read it.

- Create a mural or collage exploring the story and lessons that come from it. This mural or collage can tell the story in pictures and bas-relief.

- Read one of the stories with a strong moral lesson, such as the French story, **Earth Words,** or the Jewish story, **The Garden of Wisdom.** What would you have done if you were in the story? Why would you have done so? What will you do differently in your life now because of what you learned in the story?

- Design a helpful activity/service that you can perform in the local community based on one or more of the lessons from a story.

- Choose a real-life event or issue that is similar to one found in a story. Discuss this with others. Try to come to an agreement on what you consider to be a good way to approach the real-life issue, one that takes care of both Earth and humankind.

- Find someone who knows children living in the part of the world from which a story comes. Exchange letters, photographs and stories with a child from that culture.

- Find people living in your community who are from, or have visited, the part of the world the story you are reading is from, and who are willing to be interviewed. Think of questions to ask, then use those questions to interview those people. In

179

each case, if the person is willing, record the interview with a tape recorder or video camera. Otherwise, record the interview in a notebook.

- Compare different cultures. Play some of their music, look at some of their arts and crafts, learn about their religious beliefs and compare them. How are they similar? In what ways are they different? Why do you think they developed the way they did?
- Search the stories in this book for the appearance of the number four and the number seven. Why do you think these numbers are so important? What do they mean in those stories? Look for these numbers in other stories you read. What other numbers do you find in the stories of this book? Do any of *these* numbers appear in more than one story? What do you think is the meaning of these numbers?
- Write a story/description of what it would have been like to grow up in the culture that a story comes from and during the historical period in which the story takes place.
- Find and share with others a story from the culture(s) that is in your family. Write this story out in your own words. Combine this story with those of other people you know. Copy and bind these into a book. Make a copy for each person whose story is included in the book.
- Learn a few words of greeting and conversation from the culture represented by a particular story.
- Create art that is inspired by a story, such as poetry, illustrations, music and sculpture. Poems can be written or typed to take the shape of a plant, animal, building or some other image that you choose from that story.
- Make a mobile from art or paper sculpture inspired by one or more of these stories.
- Celebrate a specific culture that a story comes from with recipes and meals, music, art, literature and so on.
- Play games that originated in the different countries from which the stories come.
- Share a story with others. Take turns pantomiming a character, plant or animal from the story while others try to figure out who or what is being pantomimed. Play charades in a similar fashion.
- Create word jumbles and crossword puzzles with the names, places and memorable events from a particular story. Share that story with others, then have them solve the word puzzles you have designed.
- Create crafts based on the kinds of things that would be found in the culture and time period from which a story comes, such as pottery, weavings, illustrations, jewelry and models of buildings.
- Design a "true/false" or "fill-in-the-blank" quiz with questions about the characters and events in a story. Share a story, then have others complete the quiz to see how well they were listening.
- Create a maze depicting the events in a story in chronological order. Share a story, then have the listeners complete the maze.
- Create a historical time line on a wall. Place these stories along that time line in the order in which you think they ought to appear. Why do you think the stories appear in this order? What did you use in each story to help you figure out what time period that story comes from?
- Search other books for stories from the cultures that are represented in this book.

180

Sources & Author's Notes

INTRODUCTION

The Most Beautiful Bird is retold from an Italian tale passed down to me from my mother, Esther (Martone) Caduto, who learned it from her mother, Elvira Martone, who came to the United States in 1918. The exact place of origin in Italy is uncertain. My grandmother came from an orphanage in Rome, in the Province of Lazio. Her husband, Salvatore Martone, was from the small village of Santa Ambrogio sul Gonigliano, near Monte Cassino in southern Lazio. Many of the people on my mother's side of the family have a deep connection with the natural world.

I. EARTH

Origin of the Ocean is retold from *Folk Literature of the Guajiro Indians* by Johannes Wilbert and Karin Simoneau (eds.) (Los Angeles: UCLA Latin American Center Publications, 1986), pp. 51–52; and from *Indians on Horseback* by Gustaf Bolinder (London: Dennis Dobson, 1957), pp. 161–163.

This story is part of a longer creation story, "The Flood and the First Indian."

The Coming of Earth is retold from *James Mooney's History, Myths and Sacred Formulas of the Cherokees* by James Mooney (Washington, D.C.: Bureau of American Ethnology, 1891 and 1900; reissued by Historical Images of Asheville, North Carolina, 1992), pp. 239–240; from *The Path to Snowbird Mountain* by Tsisghwanai (Traveler Bird) (New York: Farrar, Straus & Giroux, 1972), pp. 12–15; and from *The Cherokee* by Theda Purdue (New York: Chelsea House, 1989), p. 13.

This version of the Cherokee Creation story comes from the eastern band. In some forms, the mountains are shaped by the wings of a buzzard. In the version used here, which was originally called, "How the World Was Made," the water beetle is of the genus *Gyrinus*, and is called the "mellow bug" or "apple beetle" by locals. In another version, the water spider, *Dolomedes*, helps bring Earth up from the ocean bottom.

The Earthquake Fish is retold from *Japanese Fairy World* by William Elliot Griffis (Schenectady, N.Y.: James H. Barhyte, 1880), pp. 223–226.

The original verse at the end of this story is based on a traditional poem.

Earth Words is translated and retold from *Le Trésor des Contes* by Henri Pourrat (Paris: Gallimard, 1953), pp. 181–182. This is the fourth of Pourrat's seven-volume collection of French folktales. An English translation can be found in *French Folktales* by Henri Pourrat (New York: Pantheon Books, 1989), pp. 86–87. The tale also appears in another edition of *Le Trésor des Contes*, in the volume titled *Les Fées (Fairy Enchantments)* by Henri Pourrat (Paris: Editions Gallimard, 1983), p. 452.

Earth Words appears in its original form as "Le Conte Du Secret de la Fougère" ("The Story of the Secret of the Ferns"). This remarkable tale speaks of how the power of ferns, sage and other plants could be of immense help to us, "If only we knew how to see green things."

II. SKY

Why the Sky Is High is retold from *Myths & Legends of the Polynesians* by Johannes Carl Andersen (London: George G. Harrap & Co, Ltd., 1928), pp. 192, 222–228. Another version is found in *The World of the Polynesians* by Antony Alpers (Aukland, N.Y.: Oxford University Press, 1987), pp. 59–63.

There are two stories retold here from Mangaia. The first tells of Maui''s premature birth, of his "burial" at the seashore and of how he was resurrected and raised by the sea beings. The original sky story, "Maui' Lifts the Sky," says that the sky is "built of solid blue stone."

Hare Rescues the Sun is retold from *The Sun Maiden and the Crescent Moon: Siberian Folk Tales* by James Riordan (New York: Interlink Books, 1991), pp. 161–163.

The original Inuit (Eskimo) story, "How the Sun Was Rescued," tells of the hardships of living in the cold, long nights of Arctic winters. The hard edges of this story reveal the kinship that these people share with the Inuit and Aleut who live in the extreme cold regions of North America.

First People Make the Stars is retold from *Navaho Folk Tales* by Franc Johnson Newcomb (Albuquerque: University of New Mexico Press, 1967), pp. 82–88; from *Navajo History* by Ethelou Yazzie (ed.) (Chinle, Ariz.: Rough Rock Press, 1971), p. 21; and from *The Sacred: Ways of Knowledge, Sources of Life*, by Peggy V. Beck, Anna Lee Walters and Nia Francisco (Tsaile, Ariz.: Navajo Community College Press, 1992), pp. 87–88. I also consulted another version found in *Starlore Among the Navajo* by Berard Haile, OFM (Santa Fe, N. M.: Museum of Navajo Ceremonial Art, 1947), pp. 23–28.

This story is part of a longer creation tale, "The Sun, Moon and Stars," which also tells how Sun and Moon came to be. The lengthy original story also explains the origins of specific constellations.

The Seven Sisters is retold from *Myths & Legends of the Australian Aboriginals* by W. Ramsay Smith (New York: Farrar & Rinehart Publishers, 1930), pp. 345–350.

This story, which is originally called, "The Origin of the Pleiades," is an unusual indigenous tale that describes the rite of passage for *female* members of a culture. Although I retold the story in its entirety, I softened a few images to make them less graphic.

A Golden Angel Egg is retold from *Nine Fairy Tales by Karel Čapek, and One More Thrown in for Good Measure* by Karel Čapek

(Evanston, Ill.: Northwestern University Press, 1990), pp. 92–94.

III. FIRE

The Coming of Fire is retold from *Time Before Morning: Art and Myth of the Australian Aborigines* by Louis A. Allen (New York: Thomas Y. Crowell Co., 1975), pp. 109–113; and from *The Dreamtime* by Charles P. Mountford and Ainslie Roberts (Adelaide: Rigby Limited, 1965), p. 22. The original story is titled "The Coming of Fire: The Goorda Myth."

I found another version of this story in *Art, Myth and Symbolism: Records of the American-Australian Scientific Expedition to Arnhem Land* by Charles P. Mountford (Melbourne: Melbourne University Press, 1956), pp. 293–294.

There are several Aboriginal versions of how fire was discovered. Another interesting story tells of how water rat first made fire accidentally when sparks were created as he gnawed on the root of a gum tree. That tale is found in *Myths & Legends of the Australian Aboriginals* by W. Ramsay Smith (New York: Farrar & Rinehart Publishers, 1930), pp. 67–69.

Hippo Befriends Fire is retold from the original "Why Hippo Wears No Coat," found in *West African Folktales* by Jack Berry (Evanston, Ill.: Northwestern University Press, 1991), pp. 158–159.

Pele's Wrath of Fire is retold from *Legends of the South Seas* by Antony Alpers (New York: Thomas Y. Crowell Co., 1970), pp. 253–256; and from *Myths & Legends of the Polynesians* by Johannes Carl Andersen (London: George G. Harrap & Co, Ltd., 1928), pp. 267–268. Other sources of this story include *A Narrative of a Tour through Hawaii* by William Ellis (London: Fisher, Son and Jackson, 1826, Honolulu reprint, 1917); and *Hawaiian Folk Tales: A Collection of Native Legends* by Thomas G. Thrum et al., (ed.) (Chicago: A. C. McClurg & Co., 1907).

In Alpers' book, this story appears as "The Eruption of Pele's Anger," and in Andersen it is called "Pele the Fire Goddess." These tales are one small part of Pele's long saga, beginning with her arrival to the Hawaiian Islands and her numerous adventures, many of which explain the geologic features of the islands.

Princess Firefly's Lovers is a classic, retold from "The Fire Quest" in *Green Willow and other Japanese Fairy Tales* by James Grace (London: MacMillan and Co., Ltd., 1912), pp. 161–164; from "The Fire-Fly's Lovers" in *Japanese Fairy Tales* by William Elliot Griffis (London: George G. Harrap & Co., 1869), pp. 13–20; and from "Princess Firefly" in *Old-World Japan: Legends of the Land of the Gods* by Frank Rinder (London: George Allen, 1895), pp. 153–159.

iv. Water

Natsilane & the Killer Whales is retold from "Natsilane" in *Heroes & Heroines: Tlingit-Haida Legend* by Mary L. Beck (Anchorage: Alaska Northwest Books, 1989), pp. 3–14; from "How the Killer Whale Came to Be" in *Tlingit: Their Art, Culture & Legends* by Dan Kaiper and Nan Kaiper (Saanichton, B.C. and Seattle, Wash.: Hancock House Publisher, 1978), pp. 55–63; and from "Origin of the Killer Whale" and "Story of the Killer-Whale Crest of the Daql!awe´di" in *Tlingit Myths and Texts* by John R. Swanton (Washington, D.C.: U.S. Government Printing Office, Smithsonian Institution, Bureau of American Ethnology Bulletin 39, 1909), pp. 25–27 and pp. 230–231.

This is one of the most popular stories among the Tlingit and Haida, among whose people many belong to the crest of the Killer Whale. Success and good fortune await those who see a killer whale.

Crab & the Water Animals is retold from *Folktales of India* by Brenda E. F. Beck, Peter J. Claus, Praphulladatta Goswami and Jawaharlal Handoo (eds.) (Chicago: University of Chicago Press, 1987), pp. 123–124.

This tale, the original of which is called, "The Origin of Different Water Animals," is a crookedly humorous story from the Naga tribesmen of northeastern India. Among other lessons that can be drawn, the fate of the minnow, shrimp and frog can be seen as a judgment by the egalitarian Naga tribe on the unfairness of the Hindu caste system, which ranks people's worth as part of a rigid hierarchy.

The Tortoise & the Egrets is retold from "The Boastful Tortoise" in *Folk Tales from China* by (anonymous) (Peking: Foreign Language Press, 1958), pp. 9–12; and from "The Geese and the Tortoise" in *The Folklore of China* by Nicholas B. Dennys (Amsterdam: Oriental Press, 1968 [original edition 1876]), p. 149. I also consulted two other versions: "The Tale of the Tortoise Who Forgot the Crane's Warning," found in *Introduction to Classic Japanese Literature* by The Kokusai Bunka Shinkokai (ed.) (The Society for International Cultural Relations: Tokyo, 1948), p. 99; and "The Fate of the Turtle" in *The Olive Fairy Book* by Andrew Lang (ed.) (New York: Dover Publications, Inc., 1907, 1934), pp. 242–246.

In its original versions, this Tibetan fable features several different kinds of birds. The three forms that I relied on the most heavliy are "The Boastful Tortoise," "The Geese and the Tortoise" and "The Tale of the Tortoise Who Forgot the Crane's Warning." There are stories from many different cultures in which birds carry a tortoise over a great distance. I must admit that I "softened" the ending a bit. In the original stories tortoise lands on a rock and is smashed to bits.

The Porpoise Wife is retold from *Tales from Ulithi Atoll* by William A. Lessa (Berkeley and Los Angeles: University of California Press, 1961), pp. 38–39.

"The Porpoise Girl," as it is originally called, is about the origin of the porpoise clans found on some of the Caroline Islands of Micronesia. In telling a story about how closely these people are "related" to the porpoises, this tale becomes the reason for the taboo that prohibits the eating of porpoise meat. This particular story is not from Ulithi—it most likely originated on the islands of Yap and Murilo. Similar stories are found throughout the world, such as the Maliseet story "The Deer Wife" from Nova Scotia, Canada, and the Celtic tale "The Secret of Roan Inish," of which there is a children's book, *The Secret of Roan Inish* by Rosalie Fry (New York: Hyperion, 1995).

Hummingbird & the Selfish Fox is retold from *Folk Literature of the Yamana Indians* by Johannes Wilbert (ed.) (Berkeley: University of California Press, 1977), pp. 89–91; from "How Táiyin Came to the Aid of the People," found in *Folk Literature of the Selknam Indians: Martin Gusinde's Collection* of *Selknam Narratives* (Latin American Studies, vol. 32) by Johannes Wilbert, (ed.) (Los Angeles: UCLA Latin American Center Publications, 1975), pp. 57–61; and another version, "The Selfish Fox," is found in *Die Feuerland-Indianer: Ergebnisse meiner vier Forschungsreisen in den Jahren 1918 bis 1924, unternommen im Auftrage des Ministerio de Instrucción Pública de Chile.* vol. I, *Die Selknam: Vom Leben und Denken eines Jägervolkes auf der grossen Feüerlandinsel* by Martin Gusinde (Mödling, Austria: 1931), p. 616.

In many tales from the Yamana of Tierra del Fuego, a smart, brave, determined hummingbird saves a community of animals, despite its small size.

V. SEASONS & WEATHER

Earth & Sky Reconcile is retold from *West African Folktales* by Jack Berry (Evanston, Ill.: Northwestern University Press, 1991), pp. 183–186.

This story is originally told as "The Quarrel Between Heaven and Earth." I have taken the lyrics of the song found within the story and transformed them into a song of rhyming verse.

Nanabozho Brings the Seasons is retold from *Nanabozho, Giver of Life* by Alethea K. Helbig (ed.) (Brighton, Mich.: Green Oak Press, 1987), pp. 200–201; and from *The Nishnawbe News*, vol. 5, no. 3 (Nov. 1977): 7, published by the Organization of North American Indian Students, Northern Michigan University, Marquette, Michigan.

In its original form, this story is called "The Seasons." Some readers will recognize Nanabozho as the trickster hero who goes by many names, including Nanibojo, Manabozho, Manabus, Wenibojo and Wisakejak. These names refer to the powerful, beloved Anishinabe figure as "foolish fellow," "great rabbit" or "old man." Nanabozho can at times be foolish or wise, a mischievous trickster or a benevolent creative force.

Rainbow is retold from *The Way of the Dead Indians: Guajiro Myths and Symbols* by Michel Perrin (Austin: University of Texas Press, 1987), pp. 54–55; and from *Folk Literature of the Toba Indians*, vol. 2, by Johannes Wilbert and Karin Simoneau (Los Angeles: UCLA Latin American Center Publications, 1989), p. 75.

There are many versions of this story, including "Rainbow" in which the rainbow is the tongue of a snake, and "The Rainbow and the Crocodile."

The Wrath of March is retold from *Tales Merry and Wise* by Rose Laura Mincieli (New York: Henry Holt & Co., 1958), pp. 107–110; and *Italian Folktales* by Italo Calvino (New York: Pantheon Books, 1980), pp. 703–704.

In both original versions of this story, Mincieli's "The Capricious Month" and Calvino's "March and the Shepherd," March addresses his sister, April, in verse. I have created an original version of this verse, and I have added a poetic reply from April. A French version of this tale is found in *Les Contes Populaires de L'ile de Corse*, vol. XVI, "Les Littératures Populaires de Toutes les Nations" by Jean Baptiste Frédéric Ortoli (Paris: Maisonneuve et Cie, 1883).

A Basket of Friendship is retold from *The Moons of Korea* by Kim Yong Ik (Seoul: Korean Information Service, Inc., 1959), pp. 47–50.

"A Basketful of Happiness," as it is originally called, helps us to see how difficulties and harsh weather enrich our lives and strengthen the ties between people. In addition, this story is a metaphor for the possibility of peace in a long-troubled land.

VI. PLANTS

The Bay-Tree Girl is retold in part from *Modern Greek Folktales* by Richard McGillivray Dawkins (London: Oxford at the Clarendon Press, 1953), pp. 136–139. I have also drawn from the Kálymnos version, "The Girl in the Bay-Tree," found in *Forty-Five Stories from the Dodekanese* by Richard McGillivray Dawkins (Cambridge, England: Cambridge University Press, 1950), no. 16, pp. 207–211; from the version from *Folk-Lore of Modern Greece: The Tales of the People* by Edmund Martin Geldart (London: W. Swan Sonnenschein & Co., 1884), pp. 85–87; and from the version translated from Greek in *Contes Populaires Grecs* by Jean Pio (Copenhagen: Andr.-Fréd. Høst & Sons, Publishers, 1879), pp. 72–74.

Kospi & the First Flowers is retold from *Folk Literature of the Tehuelche Indians* by Johannes Wilbert and Karin Simoneau (eds.) (Los Angeles: UCLA Latin American Center Publications, 1984), pp. 120–121. An early version is found in *Joiuen Tsoneka (Leyendas Tehuelches)* by Mario Echeverría Baleta (Río Gallegos: Talleres Gráficos Noguera, 1977), p. 35.

The original version, "Kospi," is very simple and spare. I have added some blush to the petals.

Befriended by Flowers is retold from *Under the Starfruit Tree: Folktales from Vietnam* by Alice M. Terada (Honolulu: University of Hawaii Press, 1989), pp. 95–98; and from the original version translated from Vietnamese and Chinese, which can be found in *Tän-Biên Truyên-Ky Man Luc* by Nguyen Tu (Hanoi: Bô Giáo-Duc, Ministry of Education, Center for Educational Materials, 1970), pp. 79–113.

The Vietnamese version of this lovely story, "West Garden Wall Encounter," includes pages of poetic exchange between the young man and the two young women. To reflect this, I added the verses of poetry and the ending touch of having the flower petals lifted by a warm breeze, then turning into butterflies. This story reveals the close, spiritual relationship many people feel to the plant world, flowers in particular, and the connection between flowers and romantic love. In Vietnam, the writing of poetry is a respected pursuit of the student of Life.

The Coming of Seeds & Gardens is retold from *Folk Literature of the Chorote Indians* by Johannes Wilbert and Karin Simoneau (eds.) (Los Angeles: UCLA Latin American Center Publications, 1985), pp. 55–56, 60–65; and from Folk Literature of the Guajiro Indians by Johannes Wilbert and Karin Simoneau (eds.) (Los Angeles: UCLA Latin American Center Publications, 1986), pp. 248–250. This tale is the synthesis of several short tales that include parts of this story. "Moon Shows Armadillo the Properties of His Plants," "Moon Reveals the Plant Cycle of a Shaman" and "Fox Causes Sowing and Harvesting to Be No Longer Simultaneous" are from several sources prepared by Alejandra Siffredi, "Temporalidad y Espacio en la Cosmovisión Chorote Montaraz" (Universidad de Buenos Aires: Doctoral Thesis, 1982); and "La

Autoconciencia de las Relaciones Sociales Entre Los Yojwáha-Chorote," in *Scripta Ethnologica*, 1(1):71–103, 1973. Two other sources, by Celia Olga Mashnshnek, are "Armadillo and His Fields" from "Algunos Personajes de la Mitología Chorote," in *Relaciones* (n.s.) 6:142–143, 1972; and "Fox and Armadillo Sow" from "La Economía de los Chorote del Chaco Central: Algunos Aspectos Mítico-religiosos de la Producción," in *Relaciones* (n.s.) 7:61, 1973.

An Elfin Harvest is retold from "The Haug-Folk Help a Man" in *Folktales of Norway* by Reidar Thorwald Christiansen (ed.) (Chicago: University of Chicago Press, 1964), pp. 96–98; and from "Fairies Assist a Farmer in His Work," in *The Migratory Legends* by Reidar Thorwald Christiansen (Helsinki: Suomalainen Tiedeakatemia/Academia Scientiarum Fennica, 1958), no. 6035, p. 167. This last version was originally collected by Ivar Aasen in Hosanger (western Norway) in about 1860, published in a newspaper in Dölen in that year, then retold in *Norske Folkeminnelags Skrifter*, I (1923): 55–58. Similar versions of this tale appeared in this same newspaper at various times: vol. 21, p. 4; vol. 38, p. 115; vol. 48, p. 85. I also consulted a recent, brief version, "The Harvesters," in *Scandinavian Folk & Fairy Tales* by Claire Booss (ed.) (New York, Avenel Books, 1984), pp. 293–294.

VII. ANIMALS

How Lion Lost the Power of Flight is retold from *African Folktales: Traditional Stories of the Black World* by Roger D. Abrahams (New York: Pantheon Books, 1983), pp. 83–86.

In my retelling, I have kept Oom Leeuw's, the Lion's, "iron" claws, as described in the original story, "The Flying Lion." The story never answers the mystery of why Oom Leeuw loses the ability to fly when Bullfrog crushes the bones in his lair.

Abu l'Hssein, the Generous is retold from *Arab Folk Tales* by Inea Bushnaq (ed.) (New York: Pantheon Books, 1986), p. 219.

As I retold the original story, "The Hospitality of Abu L'Hssein," the lesson learned by Fox grew from that of respect for Raven to an increased understanding of how Raven, in his own way, is well adapted for survival.

185

Mighty Tiger & the Hare is retold from *Mythology and Folklore of the Hui, A Muslim Chinese People* by Shujiang Li and Karl W. Luckert (Albany: State University of New York Press, 1994), pp. 431–432; from *Hindu Literature* by Epiphanius Wilson (New York: The Colonial Press, 1900), pp. 45–46; and from *The Panchatantra* by Frank Edgerton (transl.) (London: George Allen and Unwin Ltd., 1965), pp. 45–46.

The original Hui tale, "The Tiger and the Hare," was recorded in Ningxia in 1982. This story, however, has ancient roots. The version found in *Hindu Literature*, "The Story of the Lion and the Old Hare," comes from *The Book of Good Counsels*, a traditional source of Hindu wisdom. This is one of many stories found worldwide in which a smaller trickster animal— such as hare, crow, turtle or raven— outwits a creature of much greater physical power.

The First Bats is retold from *The Bird Who Cleans the World and other Mayan Fables* by Victor Montejo (Willimantic, Conn.: Curbstone Press, 1991), pp. 31–34.

Many stories describe where bats first came from. Most of them involve a transformation to or from the form of a bird. This Jakaltec-Maya story, however, "From Mouse to Bat," is most unique in the events leading up to the coming of bats.

Hedgehog Races Deer is retold from *Folktales of Germany* by Kurt Ranke (ed.) (Chicago: University of Chicago Press, 1966), p. 23. There is a seemingly endless number of race stories in which the slower animal gets help from its friends and relatives, all of which look similar in appearance. Other sources I drew from are the Bondei story, "The Tortoise and the Falcon," in *African Folktales: Traditional Stories of the Black World* by Roger D. Abrahams (New York: Pantheon Books, 1983), pp. 75–78; "Steenbuck and Tortoise" in *Myths and Legends of Botswana, Lesotho and Swaziland* by Jan Knappert (Leiden, The Netherlands: E. J. Brill, 1985), pp. 235–236; "The Whale and the Sea Slug" in *Folktales of Japan* by Keigo Seki (ed.) (Chicago: University of Chicago Press, 1956), pp. 23–24; "The Deer and the Turtle" in *Folk Literature of the Gê Indians* by Johannes Wilbert and Karin Simoneau (eds.) (Los Angeles: UCLA Latin American Center Publications, 1978),

pp. 259–260; "Deer and Turtle" in *Folk Literature of the Guajiro Indians* by Johannes Wilbert and Karin Simoneau (eds.) (Los Angeles: UCLA Latin American Center Publications, 1986), pp. 191–193; "The Rabbit and the Terrapin Race," "The Terrapin and the Deer Race" and "The Terrapin and the Fox Race" in *Friends of Thunder* (Cherokee Stories) by Jack F. Kilpatrick and Anna G. Kilpatrick (Dallas: Southern Methodist University Press, 1964), pp. 17–19; and "The Race of the Fox and the Turtle" in *Nanabozho; Giver of Life* by Alethea K. Helbig (ed.) (Brighton, Mich.: Green Oak Press, 1987), p. 127.

Whither the Animals' Freedom? is retold from *The Gypsy and the Bear* by Lucia Merecka Borski (Szczepanowicz) and Kate B. Miller (New York: Longmans, Green and Co., 1933), pp. 15–21.

This wonderful tale from Poland was originally called "How the Animals Lost Their Freedom." It has a distinctly European feeling to it, with the freedom of the animals being preserved on parchment scrolls. It is interesting how the animals' own actions are responsible for bringing about their loss of freedom. Another interesting, closely related story is "How Some Wild Animals Became Tame Ones" in *The Brown Fairy Book* by Andrew Lang (ed.) (New York: Dover Publications, 1965), pp. 197–201.

VIII. CIRCLE OF LIFE

First People: Children of the Macaques is retold from *South of the Clouds: Tales from Yunnan* by Lucien Miller (ed.) (Seattle & London: University of Washington Press, 1994), p. 77; and from the original version translated from Chinese, which is found in *Lisuzu Minjian Gushi Xuan (Anthology of Lisu Folktales)* by the Lisu Folk Story Editorial Group in Lujian (Kunming, China: Yunnang People's Publishing House, 1984), p. 3.

Although this heartrending story tells of the coming of the cycle of birth and death, its original title is "The Macaques Give Birth to the Human Race."

Death Becomes Final is retold from *Folk Literature of the Caduveo Indians* by Johannes

Wilbert and Karin Simoneau (eds.) (Los Angeles: UCLA Latin American Center Publications, 1989), pp. 36–37; and from another version translated from Portuguese found in *Religião e Mitologia Kadiuéu* by Darcy Ribeiro (Rio de Janeiro: Ministério da Agricultura, Conselho Nacional de Proteção aos Índios, Serviço de Proteção aos Índios, 1950), publication no. 106, p. 144.

This sad, beautiful story, which is originally called "The Origin of Death," is rich in symbols. The red lily is Caracará's heart, upon which the loss of his mother pulls so strongly. The story may also be called "The Origin of Compassion." Indeed, there are other stories about the finality of death that caution that, if everyone lived forever, we would lose our feelings of compassion for one another and our sense of appreciation for what we share in life.

Magpie & the Bird Nests is retold from *English Fairy Tales* by Joseph Jacobs (New York: G.P. Putnam's Sons, 1891), pp. 195–197.

The original tale is called "The Magpie's Nest." The European blackbird that appears in this story is, in figure and habit, closely related to the American robin.

The Caprice of Heron & Crane is retold from *Siberian and Other Folktales* by C. Fillingham Coxwell (London: The C.W. Daniel Co., 1925), pp. 783–785; from *Russian Fairy Tales* by Alexsandr Nikolaevich Afanas'ev (New York: Pantheon, 1945), p. 66; and from *Words of Wisdom: Russian Folk Tales* by Alexander Afanasiev (Moscow: Raduga Publishers, 1987), pp. 6–8. Other versions are found in *Zoological Mythology, or the Legends of the Animals* by Angelo De Gubernatis (London: Trubner & Co., 1872), p. 261; and in *Russian Popular Tales* by Alexandr Nikolaevich Afanasief (2nd edition, 1873, and 4th edition, 1913), no. 36.

The original story, "The Heron and Crane," was written in verse. I retained the story in its entirety, but recreated it in prose. It comes from Vologda, more than 320 kilometers (200 miles) northeast of Moscow. Other versions are known as "The Heron and the Crane" and "The Crane and the Heron."

IX. STEWARDSHIP

Disappearing Flowers is retold from *Arab Folk-Tales* by Inea Bushnaq (ed.) (New York: Pantheon Books, 1986), pp. 104–108.

The tale I have told is part of a longer story, "Flowers That Vanished in the Night." In the original version, the prince who rescues the princess from the Marid has further adventures during which the black ram carries him down through the seven levels of Earth to the underworld. There, he slays a serpent and is rescued by a griffin who flies him up through the seven levels of Earth. When the prince arrives home, he weds the princess.

Turtle Returns the Gift is retold from "The Grateful Turtle" in *Japanese Tales* by Royall Tyler (New York: Pantheon Books, 1987), pp. 152–153; from *Konjaku Monogatari-shū* by W. Michael Kelsey (transl.) (Boston: Twayne Publishers, 1982), pp. 119, 143–147; and from "Uraschimataro and the Turtle" in *The Pink Fairy Book* by Andrew Lang (New York: Dover Publications, Inc., 1967), pp. 25–32. An interesting twist on this theme is the story "How a Boy Bought Some Turtles and Set Them Free," in *A Collection of Tales from Uji: A Study and Translation of Uji Shui Monogatari* by D. E. Mills (London: Cambridge University Press, 1970), pp. 382–383. Another original version is found in *Konjaku Monogatarishū* by Yamada Yoshio, Yamada Tadao, et al. (eds.) (Tokyo: Iwanami, 1961, 1963), book 19, p. 29.

In one original story, "The Grateful Turtle," Fujiwara no Yamakage's youngest son is thrown overboard by his stepmother during the storm. After the turtle rescues his son, Yamakage encourages him toward religious life and the boy becomes a monk. Yamakage was a real person who lived from A.D. 825–889. This religious connection is also present in Kelsey's *Konjaku* version, in which the turtle saves a monk named Gusai.

The Fairy Circle is retold from *Folk Tales of Breffny* by B. Hunt (London: MacMillan and Co. Ltd., 1912), pp. 99–103 and 117–120.

"The Fairy Circle" brings together the elements of two traditional Celtic tales, "The Tillage in the Fort" and "The Cutting of the

187

Tree." A fort is a circle made by the *Tuatha de Danaan*, the Fairies. Great misfortune is said to befall anyone who disturbs a fairy circle.

The Pumpkin Seed Bird is retold from *Creole Folktales* by Patrick Chamoiseau (New York: The New Press, 1994), pp. 31–34.

This whimsical story is originally called "A Pumpkin Seed." There is also a fascinating, parallel story from Vietnam on the other side of the world. "Under the Starfruit Tree" is the title story in *Under the Starfruit Tree: Folktales from Vietnam* by Alice M. Terada (Honolulu: University of Hawaii Press, 1989), pp. 3–6. In this tale, an eagle, who perches in the starfruit tree, leaves a poor, generous young man a bar of gold. In his greed to obtain a bar of gold of his own, the young man's older brother grabs the eagle's feet. The eagle flies out over the ocean and drops the greedy brother to his death.

X. WISDOM

The Wisdom of Nature is retold from "The Lion and the Snake" in *Myths & Legends of the Swahili* by Jan Knappert (London: Heinemann Educational Books, 1970), pp. 130–131; from "The Farmer and the Leopard" in *The Rich Man and the Singer: Folktales from Ethiopia* by Mesfin Habte-Mariam (storyteller) and Christine Price (ed.) (New York: E.P. Dutton & Co., 1971), pp. 8–9; and from "The Snake Hunter" in *Fishing in Rivers of Sierra Leone Oral Literature* by Heribert Hinzen, Frederick Bobor James, Jim Martin Sorie and Sheikh Ahmed Tejan Tamu (eds.) (Freetown, Sierra Leone: People's Educational Association of Sierra Leone, 1987), p. 121.

The tale of a hunted snake, or other hunted animal, which is saved by a person or another animal, is one of the most commonly told stories in Africa. In this tale, Nature speaks its mind about humankind. It is clear at the end that nature's fate lies in human hands.

Four Who Made a Tiger is retold from *Tales of Ancient India* by J. A. B. Van Buitenen (Chicago: University of Chicago Press, 1959), pp. 51–54; from *Folktales from India* by A. K. Ramanujan (ed.) (New York: Pantheon Books, 1991), pp. 319–320; and from *Panchatantra* by Pandit Vishnu Sharma (G.L. Chandiramani, translator) (Calcutta: Rupa & Co., 1991), pp. 224–225.

In its original form, this tale is called "Four Who Made a Lion," "The Tiger-Makers" and "The Story of the Brahmins Who Put Life into the Lion," respectively. No bones about it, this graphic cautionary tale clearly shows that people have been wrestling for thousands of years with many issues that we consider to be of our times.

The Silkies & the Fisherman's Sons is retold from *The Broonie, Silkies & Fairies: Travellers' Tales* by Duncan Williamson (Edinburgh: Canongate Publishing, Ltd., 1985), pp. 109–117.

This story, originally called "The Fisherman and His Sons," comes from Argyll on the Highlands in the West Coast of Scotland, about 75 kilometers (47 miles) northwest of Glasgow. It is a story often told by the Gypsies. These folk are also known as Travellers, a name that is not burdened by the many false stereotypes that many associate with "Gypsy."

The Garden of Wisdom is retold from *The Folklore of the Jews* by Angelo S. Rappoport (London: The Soncino Press, 1937), pp. 235–239. An earlier version in Hebrew is found in *Meil Zedaka* by Eliahu Cohen (Smyrna [Turkey], 1721), pp. 24 a–b.

Few tales show so clearly how timeless are the moral struggles with which humankind wrestles. "The Journey of the Three Princes," as it is originally called, reminds us that we can seek wisdom and virtue in the natural wonders and mysteries of Creation.

FIRST TAIL, LAST TALE

Tell Tails is retold from *The Bird Who Cleans the World and other Mayan Fables* by Victor Montejo (Willimantic, Conn.: Curbstone Press, 1991), p. 51.

I found many stories about animals' tails. This Mayan story, "The Tail of the Dog," is a most endearing place to end our journey together.

Permissions

I am grateful to the following people and publishers for permission to include my original versions of the following tales.

"Why the Sky Is High" is retold from a story called, "Maui' Lifts the Sky," found in Johannes Carl Andersen's *Myths and Legends of the Polynesians* (1928), pp. 192 and 222–223, and is included with permission of Eric Dobby Publishing Ltd., Lane, St. Albans, England. This book was originally published by George G. Harrap & Company Ltd., London.

"Hare Rescues the Sun" is retold from a story called "How the Sun Was Rescued," found in James Riordan's *The Sun Maiden and the Crescent Moon: Siberian Folk Tales* (1991), pp. 161–163, and is included with permission of Cannongate Books Ltd., Edinburgh, Scotland, and Interlink Books, Northhampton, Massachusetts, an imprint of Interlink Publishing Group, Inc. Copyright © 1989 James Riordan.

"The Seven Sisters" is retold from a story called, "The Origin of the Pleiades," found in W. Ramsay Smith's *Myths & Legends of the Australian Aboriginals* (© 1930), pp. 345–350, published by Farrar & Rinehart Publishers, New York, and is included with permission of Harrap, Larousse PLC, London, and Henry Holt and Company, Inc., New York. This book was originally published by George C. Harrap & Company Ltd., London.

"A Golden Angel Egg" is retold from a portion of an old Czech folktale, "The Bird's Tale," found in Karel Čapek's *Nine Fairy Tales by Karel Čapek, and One More Thrown in For Good Measure* (1990), pp. 92–94, and is included with permission of the publisher, Northwestern University Press, Evanston, Illinois. All rights reserved. English translation copyright © 1990 Dagmar Herrmann.

"Hippo Befriends Fire" and "Earth & Sky Reconcile" are retold from two stories, "Why Hippo Wears No Coat" and "The Quarrel Between Heaven and Earth," collected and translated by Jack Berry and first published in *West African Folktales*, pp. 158–159, 183–186. Copyright ©1991 by Northwestern University Press. All rights reserved. These stories are included with permission of Northwestern University Press, Evanston, Illinois.

"Crab & the Water Animals" is retold from a story called, "The Origin of Different Water Animals," found in Brenda E.F. Beck, Peter J. Claus, Praphulladatta Goswami and Jawaharlal Handoo's (eds.), *Folktales of India* (1987), pp. 123–124, and is included with permission of the University of Chicago Press, Chicago, Illinois.

"The Porpoise Wife" is retold from a story called, "The Porpoise Girl," found in William A. Lessa's *Tales from Ulithi Atoll: A Comparative Study in Oceanic Folklore* (1961), pp. 38–39, and is included with permission of the University of California Press. Copyright ©1961 the Regents of the University of California.

"Rainbow" is retold from a story called, "Rainbow," found in Michel Perrin's *The Way of the Dead Indians: Guarjiro Myths and Symbols* (1987), pp. 54–55, and is included with permission of the author and the University of Texas Press, Austin.

"Kospi & the First Flowers" is retold from a story called, "Kospi," found in Johannes Wilbert and Karin Simoneau's (eds.), *Folk Literature of the Tehuelche Indians* (© 1984), pp. 120–121, and is included with permission of UCLA Latin American Center Publications, Los Angeles.

"The Coming of Seeds & Gardens" is retold from four stories found in Johannes Wilbert and Karin Simoneau's (eds.), *Folk Literature of the Chorote Indians* (© 1985), pp. 55 and 60–64, and is included with permission of UCLA Latin American Center Publications, Los Angeles.

"How Lion Lost the Power of Flight" is retold from a story called, "The Flying Lion," found in Roger D. Abrahams' *African Folktales: Traditional Stories of the Black World,* copyright © 1983 by Roger D. Abrahams, pp. 83–86, and is included with permission of Pantheon Books, a division of Random House, Inc., New York.

"Abu l'Hssein, the Generous" and "Disappearing Flowers" are retold from two stories, "The Hospitality of Abu l'Hssein" and "Flowers That Vanished in the Night," found in *Arab Folk-Tales,* copyright © 1986 by Inea Bushnaq, pp. 219 and 104–108, and are included with permission of Pantheon Books, a division of Random House, Inc., New York.

"The First Bats" and "Tell Tails" are retold from two stories called, "From Mouse to Bat" and "The Tail of the Dog," found in Victor Montejo's *The Bird Who Cleans the World and other Mayan Fables* (1991), pp. 31–34 and 51, and are included with permission of Curbstone Press, Willimantic, Connecticut.

"Whither the Animals' Freedom?" is retold from a story called, "How the Animals Lost Their Freedom," found in Lucia Merecka Borski (Szczepanowicz) and Kate B. Miller's *The Gypsy and the Bear,* copyright © 1933, 1961 by Lucia Borski and Kate B. Miller, pp. 15–21, originally published by Longmans, Green and Co., and is included with permission of David McKay Co., Inc., a division of Random House, Inc., New York.

"The Pumpkin Seed Bird" is retold from a story called, "A Pumpkin Seed," found in Patrick Chamoiseau's *Creole Folktales* (1994), pp. 31–34, and is included with permission of The New Press, New York, © 1994.

"The Silkies & the Fisherman's Sons" is retold from a story called, "The Fisherman and His Sons," found in Duncan Williamson's *The Broonie, Silkies & Fairies: Traveller's Tales* (1985), pp. 109–117, and is included with permission of Canongate Books, Ltd., Edinburgh, Scotland.

"The Garden of Wisdom" is retold from a story called, "The Journey of the Three Princes," found in Angelo S. Rappoport's *The Folklore of the Jews* (1937), pp. 235–239, and is included with permission of The Soncino Press, Ltd., New York.

Index

Here the stories are indexed (1) by title, (2) by culture and (3) by country and geographical area. In addition to these indexes, the lessons discussed at the end of each section serve as another reference source. These lessons describe many of the subjects that each story teaches about, its original culture and geographical area and about Earth.

INDEX OF STORIES BY TITLE

INDEX OF STORIES BY CULTURE

(Grouped by Continents & World Regions)

INDEX OF STORIES
BY COUNTRY
& GEOGRAPHICAL AREA
(Grouped by Continents & World Regions)